Mrs. E's Extraordinary Alphabet Activities

Written by Kathy Etringer

Illustrated by Mary Galan Rojas

Teaching & Learning Company

1204 Buchanan St., P.O. Box 10
Carthage, IL 62321-0010

This book belongs to

_____

Edited by Ellen Sussman

Copyright © 2006, Teaching & Learning Company

ISBN 13: 978-1-57310-487-6

ISBN 10: 1-57310-487-6

Printing No. 987654321

Teaching & Learning Company
1204 Buchanan St., P.O. Box 10
Carthage, IL 62321-0010

Table of Contents

Dear Teacher or Parent,

Where would we be without our alphabet—the 26 letters of the English language that combine to create our vocabulary of thousands upon thousands of words.

While most books, magazines and newspapers are printed in the 26-letter Roman alphabet, the Romans did not invent it. They did, however, put the finishing touches on a written system of communicating that had been growing for thousands of years.

The English alphabet was developed from various early writing systems that began with sign writing in ancient Egypt. By 114 A.D. the Romans had given most capital letters their current form. Interestingly, the letters J, U and W were not added to the alphabet until the Middle Ages. Lowercase letters gradually developed from capital letters, and it is said that these smaller letters were used because they saved space in books.

According to World Book Encyclopedia, the English alphabet is not well suited to writing words in English. It doesn't have a separate character for each distinctive sound in the English language, and it has several characters with more than one sound. Other languages, such as French and German, that use Roman letters use accent marks to show changes in sounds.

All this said, learning the alphabet is still a joy for children. It's usually the first skill taught in preschool and kindergarten and becomes the focus of all that a child absorbs through books and other printed material.

In Mrs. E's Extraordinary Alphabet Activities young learners are introduced to the 26 letters of the alphabet and the short and long vowel sounds. A multitude of delightful picture books, creative and multisensory hands-on activities that focus on writing, phonics, art, math and science combine to make learning the alphabet an exciting experience.

In addition to the suggested read-aloud book for each lesson, a list of other titles is included for each letter. We encourage you to fill your classroom with a variety of appropriate books when teaching each letter and sound.

Have fun planning and doing these creative lessons while building your personal read-aloud book collection to use with groups of young learners for years to come.

As you teach these new alphabet lessons, consider the fringe benefit of starting a fresh, new collection of books, a collection you'll have on hand for next year's group of young learners and those beyond.

Sincerely,

Kathy

Kathy Etringer

Activities to Help Teach the Alphabet and Letter Sounds

- As you teach each letter, have children bring items from home that begin with the letter. Make a list of the items on chart paper. Have children look at each word on the list and, for consonants, listen how each word begins with the same sound.

- Play a guessing game, "I'm thinking of . . ." In this game you think of an item that begins with a certain letter, then give clues to help children guess the object. Example: I'm thinking of something that begins with the letter F. It's green and it hops. What is it?

- Encourage children to look for letters and words they see every day by having them bring items to school that have well-recognized logos. Examples: an empty Jell-O™ box or Cheerios™ box, food labels, bags or sacks with local store names and logos. Display them on the bulletin board.

- Give children a number of opportunities to write the letters, both capital and lowercase, using different media—crayons, colored chalk, finger paint, oil pastels and tempera paints. Using bright colored chalk, write a letter or word on the chalkboard. Have a small bucket of water nearby and have a child dip his or her finger in the water and then trace over the letter or word. When the water dries, the color will be more intense, but will wash off the chalkboard easily. Children love this activity and enjoy being asked to finger trace at the chalkboard.

- Use the large classroom alphabet displayed in your room as a focal point when teaching each letter. An effective way to help children focus on the letter being learned is to frame the letter you are teaching with a bright construction paper frame. You will find that the children will begin checking the alphabet strip each day to see the letter they will be working on.

- Who has an A in their name? Who has two A's? Who has an N—or two N's together as in *Hannah*? Whose name has the most letters? Whose name has the fewest letters?

- Make a set of capital and lowercase alphabet cards. Have children match the capital letter with the correct lowercase letter.

- Write each child's first name on a note card and have him or her decorate the name. As you call out each letter of the alphabet, have each child whose name begins with that letter bring the name card to you. Display each child's name under the letter that his or her name begins with. This is an effective way to begin a word wall of names.

Additional A to Z Read-Aloud Titles

A

All About Alfie by Shirley Hughes
Alligators All Around: An Alphabet
    by Maurice Sendak
Alphabet City by Stephen T. Johnson
An Alphabet of Animals by Christopher Wormell
Ape in a Cape: An Alphabet of Odd Animals
    by Fritz Eichenberg

B

Barnyard Banter by Denise Fleming
Blueberries for Sal by Robert McCloskey
Bones, Bones, Dinosaur Bones by Byron Barton
Brown Bear, Brown Bear, What Do You See?
    by Bill Martin, Jr.
Bunches and Bunches of Bunnies
    by Louise Matthews

C

Charlie the Caterpillar by Dom DeLuise
Click, Clac, Moo—Cows That Type
    by Doreen Cronin
The Cobble Street Cousins by Cynthia Rylant
The Crazy Crawler Crane and Other Very Short
    Truck Stories by Mittie Cuetara
You Can't Catch Me by Charlotte Doyle

D

Danny and the Dinosaur by Syd Hoff
Diggers and Dump Trucks by Angela Royston
Digging Up Dinosaurs by Aliki
Duckling Days by Karen Wallace
Way Down Deep in the Deep Blue Sea
    by Jan Peck

E

Eat Your Peas, Ivy Louise by Leo Landry
Eloise by Kay Thompson
Emily's Own Elephant by Philippa Pearce
The Enormous Egg by Oliver Butterworth

F

Finding Foxes by Allison Blyler
Fire Fighter Piggy Wiggy
    by Christyan and Diane Fox
First Flight by David McPhail
Five Green and Speckled Frogs by Priscilla Burr
Fran's Flower by Lisa Bruce

G

A Gaggle of Geese by Philippa-Alys Browne
The Giving Tree by Shel Silverstein
Good Night, Gorilla by Reggy Rathmann
Goodnight, Goodnight by Eve Rice
Goodnight Moon by Margaret Wise Brown

H

Hats Hats Hats by Ann Morris
Hello, Harvest Moon by Ralph Fletcher
Henry Hikes to Fitchburg by D.B. Johnson
Horton Hatches the Egg by Dr. Seuss
Hot-Air Henry by Mary Calhoun
Under My Hood I Have a Hat by Karla Kuskin

I

I Am a Bunny by Ole Risom
If I Ran the Circus by Dr. Seuss
Iktomi and the Berries by Paul Goble
I Wish I Could Fly by Ron Maris
I Wonder If I'll See a Whale by Frances Weller

J

Jemima Puddle-Duck by Sarah Toast
Jesse Bear: What Will You Wear?
    by Nancy White Carlstrom
Josephina Hates Her Name by Diane Engel
Jungle Drum by Deanna Wundrow
Just Grandma (Grandpa) and Me
    by Mercer Mayer

TLC10487 Copyright © Teaching & Learning Company, Carthage, IL 62321-001

ty No-Pocket by Emmy Payne
evin and the School Nurse by Martine Davison
ndergarten by Natasha Wing
e Kitten Book by Jan Pfloog
oalas by Bernice Kohn Hunt

dybug, Ladybug, Where Are You?
    by Cyndy Szekeres
ntil by Robert McCloskey
o the Late Bloomer by Robert Kraus
op the Loop by Barbara Dugan
le, Lyle, Crocodile by Bernard Waber

Manatee Morning by Jim Arnosky
any Moons by James Thurber
ax and Molly's Winter
    by Ann Garrison Greenleaf
other's Day Mess by Karen Gray Ruelle
uncha! Muncha! Muncha!
    by Candace Fleming
ne Monday Morning by Uri Shulevitz

ana Upstairs & Nana Downstairs
    by Tomie dePaola
New Coat for Anna by Harriet Ziebert
e Night Before Kindergarten by Natasha Wing
Nap by Eve Bunting
Peas for Nellie by Chris L. Demarest
ot a Nibble! by Elizabeth Honey

ur Old House by Susan Vizurraga
ver the Moon by Rachel Wail
ver Under by Marthe Jocelyn and
    Tom Slaughter
wl Moon by Jane Yolen
wly by Mike Thaler

P

Each Peach, Pear, Plum
    by Janet and Allan Ahlberg
Lilly's Purple Plastic Purse by Kevin Henkes
Pal the Pony by R.A. Herman
Pete's a Pizza by William Steig
The Pig in the Pond by Martin Waddell
Sunday Potatoes, Monday Potatoes
    by Vicky Shiefman

Q

"Quack!" said the Billy-Goat by Charles Causley
Quacky Quack-Quack by Ian Whybrow
Quick as a Cricket by Audrey Wood
This Quiet Lady by Charlotte Zolotow

R

Little Red Riding Hood by the Brothers Grimm
Rabbits and Raindrops by Jim Arnosky
Raccoon On His Own by Jim Arnosky
The Rainbow Fish by Marcus Phister
Rotten Ralph by Jack Gantos

S

Sea Surprise by Leo Landry
"Slowly, Slowly, Slowly," said the Sloth
    by Eric Carle
Snowflake Bentley by Jacqueline Briggs Martin
Snow on Snow on Snow by Cheryl Chapman
Spinky Sulks by William Steig
Stone Soup: An Old Tale by Marcia Brown

T

Tacky the Penguin by Helen Lester
Teddy Bear, Teddy Bear by Steven Scott
Ten Go Tango by Arthur Dorros
Ten Little Ladybugs by Melanie Gerth
Tikki Tikki Tembo by Arlene Mosel
Today Was a Terrible Day by Patricia Reilly Giff
Twelve Tales by Hans Christian Andersen

LC10487 Copyright © Teaching & Learning Company, Carthage, IL 62321-0010

U

The Ugly Duckling by Hans Christian Andersen
Umbrella by Taro Yashima
Uncle Elephant by Arnold Lobel
Uncle Vova's Tree by Patricia Polacco
Up! by Kristine O'Connell George

V

Valentine Friends by Ann Schweninger
The Velveteen Rabbit by Margery Williams
Vera's First Day of School by Vera Rosenberry
The Very Busy Spider by Eric Carle
The Very Hungry Caterpillar by Eric Carle
The Very Quiet Cricket by Eric Carle

W

Waiting for Wings by Lois Ehlert
Watch William Walk by Ann Jonas
What Would Mama Do?
    by Judith Enderle and Stephanie Tessler
When the Wind Stops by Charlotte Zolotow
Where the Wild Things Are by Maurice Sendak

X

The Adventures of Taxi Dog
    by Debra and Sal Barracca
Fox on a Box by Phil Roxbee Cox
The Fox on the Box by Barbara Gregorich

Y

Yertle the Turtle and Other Stories by Dr. Seuss
Yoko's Paper Cranes by Rosemary Wells
Yonder by Tony Johnston
Yucka Drucka Droni
    by Eugenia and Vladmir Radunsky

Z

Zathura: A Space Adventure
    by Chris Van Allsburg
Zink the Zebra: A Special Tale by Kelly Weil
Zinnia and Dot by Lisa Campbell Ernst
Zin! Zin! Zin! A Violin by Lloyd Moss
Zoom! By Robert N. Munsch

General Alphabet Books

ABC USA by Martin Jarrie
A, B, See by Marilyn Janovitz
The Alphabet Tree by Leo Lionni
Animal ABC by Garth Williams
Animal Alphabet by Alex Lluch
Anno's Alphabet by Mitsumasa Anno
A Cow's Alfalfa-Bet by Woody Jackson
The Disappearing Alphabet by Richard Wilbur
Eating the Alphabet by Lois Ehlert
A Gardener's Alphabet by Mary Azarian
Journey Around New York from A to Z by
    Martha Zschock and Heather Zschock
Merriam-Webster's Alphabet Book
    by Ruth Heller
Nedobeck's Alphabet Book by Don Nedobeck
On Market Street by Arnold Lobel
The New Alphabet of Animals
    by Christopher Wormell
The Turn-Around, Upside Down Alphabet Book
    by Lisa Campbell Ernst

TLC10487 Copyright © Teaching & Learning Company, Carthage, IL 62321-0010

A is for Alligator

Aa

Before the Lesson

Reproduce copies of "There's an Alligator Under My Bed" on page 10.

Have on Hand

pencils
crayons

Read Aloud

There's an Alligator Under My Bed
   by Mercer Mayer

Talk About

Using items at hand, review the concept of *subtraction* with the children. Introduce how to create subtraction sentences by writing on the chalkboard:

___ - ___ = ___

Tell children they will be illustrating subtraction by drawing alligators under a bed, then crossing some out.

Kids Create

• Each child draws a bed as wide as the paper, leaving room to draw alligators under the bed.

• Children draw any number of alligators.

• Using a black crayon, children cross out some alligators.

• Work one-on-one with each child to write their individual subtraction sentence.

There's an Alligator Under My Bed

A is for **A**nteater

Aa

Before the Lesson

Reproduce "The anteater ate_____." sentence strip and pattern on page 12 for each child.

Have on Hand

copies of anteater pattern on page 12
12" x 18" construction paper
scrap paper
wide rubber bands cut open
crayons
scissors
glue

Read Aloud

The Icky Sticky Anteater by Dawn Bentley

Talk About

Have children listen for the short a sound in *anteater*. Then have them think of funny items the anteater would eat.

Kids Create

• Color and cut out anteaters.

• Glue an anteater on a larger piece of construction paper.

• Use scrap paper and crayons to draw food an anteater will eat, then glue it on the larger paper.

• Glue a rubber band (tongue) from the anteater's mouth to the "food."

• Help children finish the sentence and glue on the paper.

• Write capital A's and lowercase a's on the paper.

The anteater ate _____.

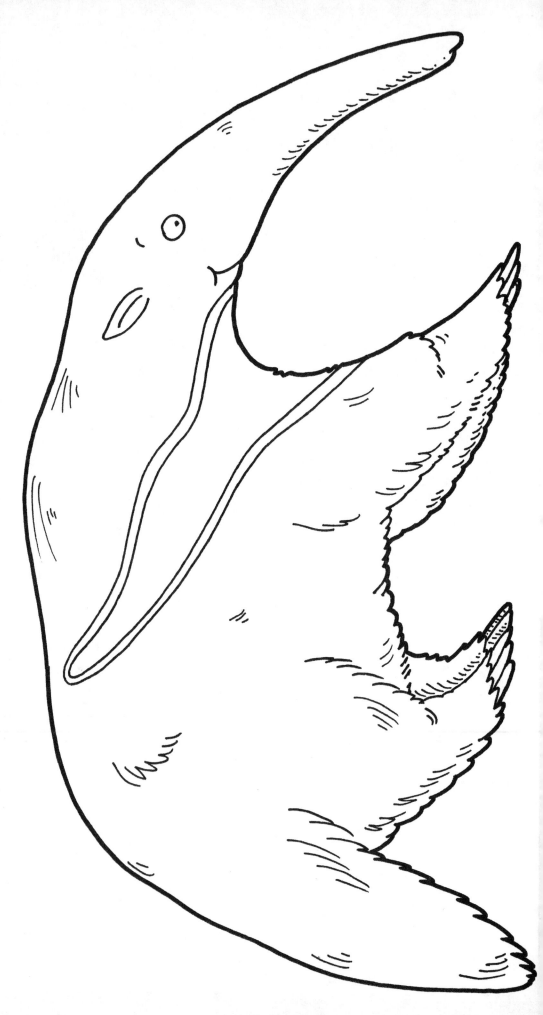

12

Before the Lesson

- Write the four-line rhyme from page 14 on chart paper.
- Write *The Magic Hat* on the front of each folder.
- Place one hat, a copy of the four-line rhyme and a folder into each canvas or zip-top bag.

Have on Hand

variety of types of hats with items hidden underneath (baseball cap, beret, cowboy hat, winter hat, etc.)
chart paper
marker
3-4 take-home canvas or quart size zip-top bags
3-4 pocket folders for sending letters home to families
stapler
reproduced copies of letter to parents

Read Aloud

The Magic Hat by Mem Fox

Talk About

Say five to six words with the short a sound: *fat, bag, can, have, planet* and *ran*. Ask children to listen for the short a sound in the middle of *magic* and *hat*.

Review the repeating phrase from the story with children. Tell children that the magic hat is going to cover up some items and they will get to guess what those items are. Teach the rhyme:

> Oh, the magic hat, the magic hat!
> It moved like this; it moved like that!
> It spun through the air and over a ____,
> And covered up _____.

Kids Create

- Children take turns taking a bag with a hat home.
- Children work with their families to find objects that fits under the hat.
- Fill in the rhyme at home. Return the hat to class and set it on a desk or table with the item from home hidden under it, covering it completely.
- Read the poem leaving out the last word. Have children guess what is hidden under the hat.

Dear Parents and Families,

Please help your child find an object that will fit under the enclosed "Magic Hat." Then have your child think of a word that rhymes with the object.

Help your child complete the rhyming verse below. Write the rhyming word on the first blank. Write the name of the object on the second blank.

Thank you for helping us with our Magic Hat game.

Sincerely,

Oh, the magic hat, the magic hat!

It moved like this; it moved like that!

It spun through the air and over a _____,

And covered up a _____.

Child's name: _____

A is in sn**a**ke

Aa

Before the Lesson

Set up a table where children can bring items or pictures that have the long a sound.

Have on Hand

cards with pictures of items with the long a sound
copy of snake pattern on page 16 for each child

Read Aloud

DK Readers: Slinky, Scaly Snakes by Jennifer A. Dussling

Talk About

Say several words with the long a sound: *snake, play, paper, clay, late, April* and *May*. Ask children to think of other words with the long a sound. Hold up picture cards of different items; children hiss like a snake if the picture has the long a sound.

Kids Create

• Color the snake.

• Make long a words by using the letters on the worksheet. Fill in the blank spaces to make six words.

• Read each long a word to a friend.

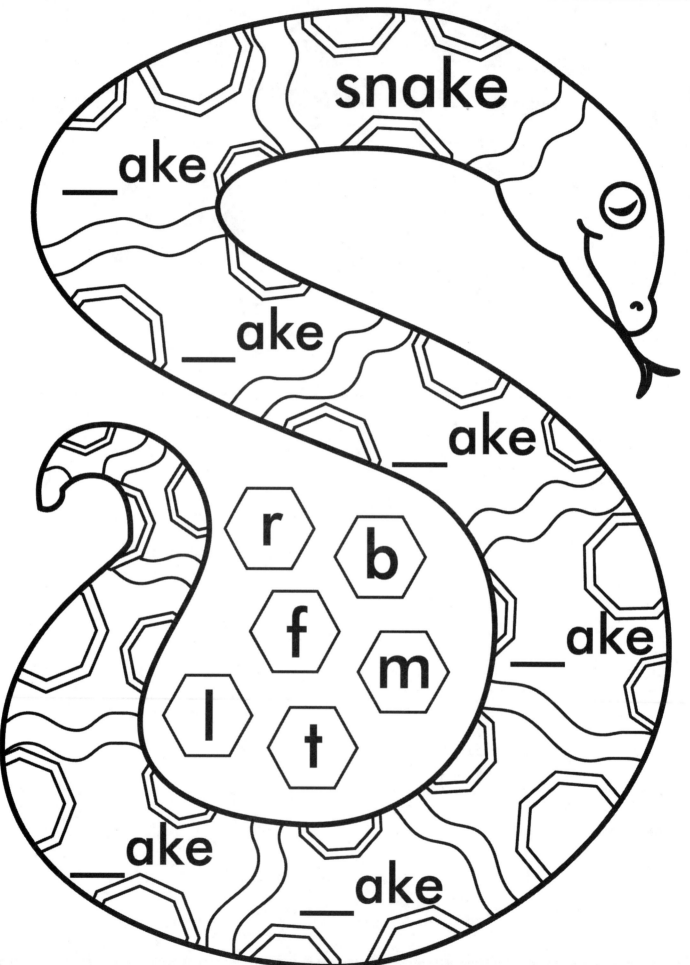

snake

__ake

__ake

__ake

r

b

f

m

l

t

__ake

__ake

__ake

16

B is for Beaver

Bb

Before the Lesson

Back a bulletin board with light blue paper that will serve as water for the display.

Have on Hand

white construction paper cut into 3" x 6" strips
brown construction paper for creating a beaver lodge
pencils
crayons
scissors
markers

Read Aloud

Beavers Beware by Barbara Brenner
Busy Beavers by Lydia Dabcovich

Talk About

Using the illustrations and photos in the books, have children describe the physical characteristics of beavers. Review factual information learned from the stories.

Kids Create

• Children each draw, color and cut out a beaver.

• Cut strips to be used for the beaver lodge using brown construction paper.

• Tell one fact they learned about beavers. Write the fact on a 3" x 6" strip of white paper and place it next to the child's beaver on the bulletin board.

As children hand in their brown strips and beavers, begin building the bulletin board display. Build a beaver lodge from the brown strips. Using a marker, draw a tunnel for beavers to follow. Place beavers in various places on the bulletin board—some in the lodge, others in the tunnel or swimming in the water.

Beavers build their homes in the water.

B is for King **B**idgood

Bb

Before the Lesson

Reproduce the tub pattern on page 19 for each child.

Have on Hand

9" x 12" colored and white construction
 paper
photo of each child
paint and small round sponges
crayons
pencils
scissors
glue

Read Aloud

King Bidgood's in the Bathtub
 by Audrey Wood

Talk About

Review the story with the children and
have them listen for the repeating phrase.

Kids Create

• Using circular-shaped sponges, paint
 circles (bubbles) onto white construction
 paper.

• Using crayons, decorate the bathtub
 and cut it out.

When painted bubbles have dried, glue
the paper behind the bathtub with
bubbles facing forward. Glue the child's
photo onto bubble paper. Round off the
edges of the bubble paper.

Help! Help!
_____Johnny___'s in the
bathtub and won't get out!
Who knows what to do?

Help! Help!

_____'s in the bathtub and won't get out!

Who knows what to do?

B is for **B**umpy
Bus Ride

Bb

Before the Lesson

Prepare strips for each child that say:
"_____ are on my bus.
They are going _____."

Cut out each child's face from a photo to use as the bus driver.

Have on Hand

9" x 12" construction paper
black construction paper cut into 4"
    squares
photo of each child
crayons
scissors

Read Aloud

The Very Bumpy Bus Ride
    by Michaela Muntean

Talk About

Ask children to pretend they are bus drivers. Have them imagine who is riding on their bus and think about where it is going. Children share their thoughts aloud.

Kids Create

• Children draw a bus, then color and cut it out.

• Draw passengers that can be seen through windows on the bus.

• Cut two black wheels from black paper squares and glue the top of the wheels to the bottom of the bus.

• Glue on the face photo for the driver.

• Fill in the blanks on the writing strip and attach it to the bus.

_____Sharks_____ are on my bus.
They are going __to the ocean__.

C is for Cactus

Cc

Before the Lesson

Create and duplicate a sentence strip for each child: "_____ birds live in my cactus hotel."

Have on Hand

9" x 12" blue and green construction paper
scraps of colored construction paper
toothpicks broken in half
crayons
sand

Read Aloud

Cactus Hotel by Brenda Z. Guiberson

Talk About

Review the animals that lived in the cactuses/cacti.

Kids Create

• Children draw a cactus on green construction paper and cut it out.

• Draw holes on the cactus for birds to live in.

• Glue the cut-out cactus onto blue construction paper.

• Use paper scraps to make birds and glue the birds by the holes.

• Glue on toothpicks to represent cactus spines.

• Spread glue on the bottom of the paper and sprinkle sand on it.

• Fill in the number, or number word, of birds on the sentence strip.

C is for Cookies

Cc

Before the Lesson

Send a letter home to parents asking if they would like to donate a package of store-bought sugar cookies for a learning lesson.

Cover a table to be used for frosting the cookies.

Counting by fives, write one number on a card until you have one card for each child.

Have on Hand

plain sugar cookies
decorating gel and frosting
plastic knives
paper plates
blank white cards
camera

Read Aloud

Cookie Count: A Tasty Pop-Up
   by Robert Sabuda

Talk About

Invite children to talk about their favorite cookies. Discuss varieties, flavors, types of filling or frosting, the reasons for their favorites. Practice counting by fives.

Kids Create

- Children each put a thin layer of frosting on a sugar cookie.

- Each child picks a number card and writes that number on his or her cookie using decorating gel.

- When children have finished, help them line up in numerical order starting with number 5.

- Starting with 5, each child calls out his or her number.

- Who can count by fives to 30 by themselves? Who can count to 40 by fives? To 50?

- As an extra learning activity, take a photo of each child holding his or her number cookie. Display it on a bulletin board to give children more practice counting by fives.

C is for Crocodile

Cc

Before the Lesson

Set up an artwork area for the children to work in small groups.

Have on Hand

9" x 12" white construction paper
scraps of white paper for teeth
copy of two-page crocodile patterns on
    pages 24-25 for each child
crayons
scissors
pencils
glue

Read Aloud

Counting Crocodiles by Judy Sierra

Talk About

Review simple addition problems. Show how to make an addition problem using the crocodile's upper and lower teeth.

Kids Create

- Children color and cut out the crocodile patterns.
- Glue the two crocodile parts together.
- Make teeth using scraps of white paper.
- Glue teeth on the upper and lower parts of the crocodile's mouth.
- Fill in the addition number sentence by writing the number of upper teeth on the first line, the number of lower teeth on the middle line and the total number of teeth on the last line. Repeat the total number in "My crocodile has _____ teeth."

teeth.

Glue

My crocodile has

___ + ___ =

D is for Dog

Dd

Before the Lesson

Create and duplicate a sentence strip for each child:

"I named my dog _____
because _____."

Write the word *dog* on the chalkboard.

Show children how to draw an oval shape.

Have on Hand

9" x 12" construction paper
4" x 4" squares of construction paper
crayons
scissors
glue
wiggly eyes

Read Aloud

Just Dog by Hiawyn Oram

Talk About

Get a discussion going about children's pet dogs. What are their names? Talk about how some dogs are named because of their physical characteristics or behaviors. Have children tell about some funny experiences they have had with dogs.

Kids Create

- Using 9" x 12" paper, children draw a small oval for the dog's head and a large oval for the body.
- Cut out the ovals and glue the head to the body.
- Use 4" x 4" squares to cut out ears, tail and legs and glue them on.
- Glue wiggly eyes on the head.
- Write the word *dog* on the dog's body.
- Complete the sentence starter independently or with teacher help.

Before the Lesson

Cut construction paper to fit over the lid of a shoe box. Draw a doorknob on the covered lid.

Glue construction paper over the box. Place the lid on the box and stand it up so it looks like a door.

Place small objects in the box. (Perhaps a treat for the children to enjoy when the last clue is given)

Prepare chart paper with *Detectives* at the top. Write *What's Behind the Door?* on the next line.

Plan four to five clues to read to the children; one each day. Example: The items in the box are soft.

Have on Hand

small shoe box
small objects to put in the box (pencils, stickers or treats)
chart paper
markers
brown construction paper

Read Aloud

Detective Dinosaur by James Skofield

Talk About

Ask children what they think a detective does. List answers on the chalkboard. Tell children that during the week they are going to be detectives, using clues to solve the mystery of "what's behind the door."

Group Activity

• Show students the "door." Tell them they will be trying to solve the mystery of what's behind the door. Write the first clue on chart paper. Example: Clue #1—There is one for each child.

• Talk about the size of the box and the clue. Have children take turns guessing what is in the box. (Children should not use another child's idea.) List each child's answer on the chart paper.

• Add a new clue each day and review earlier clues. Invite the principal and/or a few teachers to come into the classroom to make guesses. Allow the children to change their guesses after each clue.

• On the last day, after each child has guessed, show children what is behind the door.

Before the Lesson

Along an 11" length of white paper, reproduce the following at the bottom: "Meet Daisy the Duck. Her words start with D's. When she asks for _____, give her _____ please."

Have on Hand

8½" x 11" white paper
colored construction paper cut into 1" to 2" diamond shapes
yellow or orange construction paper cut in beak shapes
crayons
pencils
scissors
glue

Read Aloud

Daisy and the Egg by Jane Simmons (companion book to *Come Along Daisy*)

Meet Daisy the Duck. Her words start with D's. When she asks for _dapples_, give her _apples_ please.

Sing

Sing the song below to the tune of "On Top of Old Smokey." Have children guess what Daisy is asking for. Invite children to come up with their own verses.

Daisy the Duck
Meet Daisy the Duck,
Her words start with D's.

When she asks for dumpkins,
Give her pumpkins, please.

When she asks for deese,
Give her cheese, please.

When she asks for dapples,
Give her apples, please.

Kids Create

- Help each child draw a pencil outline of a duck.
- Color the duck with crayons.
- Glue the diamond shapes to the outline of the duck. Glue on the beak.
- Fill in the blanks with words to finish the song, independently or with teacher assistance.

E is for Enemy Pie

Ee

Before the Lesson

Start collecting empty pie tins in advance of the lesson.

Cut out brown paper pie crusts large enough to cover pie tins.

Create a sentence strip and reproduce it for each child.
"I put _____ in my enemy pie."

Have on Hand

1 clean pie tin for each child
9" x 12" brown construction paper or
    brown wrapping paper
crayons
scissors
glue
stapler

Read Aloud

Enemy Pie by Derek Munson

Talk About

Before reading the story to the children, discuss the meaning of the word *enemy*. Show the book cover and explain that the boy is making an enemy pie. Have children share ideas of what they think the boy might put in the pie. After reading the story, tell children they will be making their own enemy pies. Allow time for children to think about what they will put in their own enemy pies.

Kids Create

- Write *Enemy Pie* on the pie crust.
- Using a stapler, help children attach the paper pie crust to the pie tins.
- Draw items in the pie, or provide magazines and have children cut and paste items to put in the pie.
- Complete the sentence strip and attach it to the bottom of the pie crust.
- Have each child share his or her enemy pie.

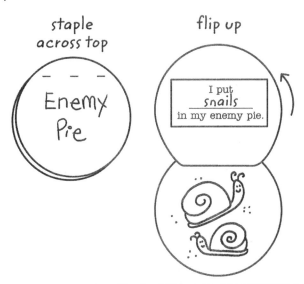

staple across top

flip up

Enemy Pie

I put
snails
in my enemy pie.

E is for **E**gg

Ee

Before the Lesson

Prepare a worksheet by writing
_____ + _____ + _____ = _____
and make a copy for each child.

Have on Hand

8¹/₂" x 14" white paper
construction paper scraps
pencils
scissors
yarn
glue
wrapping paper cut into 4" squares

Read Aloud

A Nest Full of Eggs by Priscilla Jenkins

Talk About

Encourage children to share ideas about nests, eggs and baby birds they have seen. After sharing, tell children they will be practicing how to add three numbers by making eggs and then counting them in nests. Show a sample and work through adding three numbers with the group.

Kids Create

- Children make three nests by gluing construction paper scraps on the worksheet.

- Using wrapping paper, cut out several eggs and glue them into the nests.

- Count the number of eggs in each nest and write the number on the blank beneath each nest.

- Add up all the eggs to finish the number sentence.

- Write the word *Eggs* at the top of the worksheet.

Before the Lesson

Review the concept of *subtraction* using hands-on items.

Have on Hand

five pennies for each child
pencils
crayons
copies of worksheet on page 32

Read Aloud

Benny's Pennies by Pat Brisson

Talk About

Have children listen for the short e sounds in the words *Benny's* and *pennies*. Name other words with the short e sound: *egg, elephant, bed, ten, sent* and *end*.

This lesson will be timely if children have been introduced to the concept of subtraction and have had hands-on practice.

As you read the story, talk about the items that Benny is buying. Who do the children think Benny is buying them for? After reading the story, give each child five pennies. Ask them how they would like to spend them. Work with children to illustrate subtraction number sentences. Show five pennies; take away one. How many are left? Repeat taking away two, three and four pennies in random order. Have children count their pennies to see how many are left. Name some things they could buy that have the short e sound.

Kids Create

- Children write their names to finish the title at the top of the pennies worksheet.
- Draw pictures of what they would buy.
- Cross out the number of pennies spent.
- Complete the writing activity independently or with the teacher's help.

_____'s Pennies

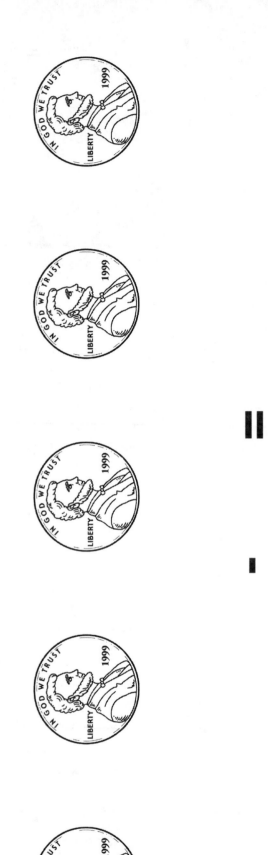

_____ - _____ = _____

I spent _____ pennies to buy _____.

E is in Sh**ee**p

easy

Ee

Before the Lesson

Reproduce the sheep pattern on page 34 on tagboard for each child.

Prepare a bulletin board with the title "My sheep says, ..."

Cut sentence strips into word bubbles, one per child.

Have on Hand

tagboard
sentence strips
small cotton balls
crayons
scissors
glue
pencil
tape

Read Aloud

Ten Sleepy Sheep by Phyllis Root
When Sheep Cannot Sleep: A Counting Book by Satoshi Kitamura

Talk About

Have children listen for the long e sound in the words *sheep* and *sleep*. Say several words and have children give you thumbs up each time they hear the long e sound in a word: *please, letter, see, apple, peanut, Easter, elephant, sneeze, season.*

Kids Create

• Children each cut out a sheep and glue cotton balls on it for a wooly coat.
• Think of a word that has the long e sound.
• Write a long e word on a word bubble.
• Add their sheep to the bulletin board with word bubbles.

34

F is for Fireflies

Ff

Before the Lesson

Create this addition template on the right side of a sheet of paper. Reproduce it for each child.

```
      _____

 +    _____

 =    _____
```

Have on Hand

white construction paper cut into 4$\frac{1}{2}$" x 6"
    pieces
yellow tempera paint
paint tins or paper cups for paint
pencils and crayons

Read Aloud

Fireflies by Julie Brinkloe
The Very Lonely Firefly by Eric Carle

Talk About

Have children share their experiences see-ing or catching fireflies. If it's summer, invite children to bring in jars with fireflies they have caught.

Kids Create

• Each child draws a jar on a piece of white construction paper and cuts it out.

• Create between four and 10 firefly lights in the jar by dipping a pinky finger in yellow paint and making fingerprints on the paper.

• After the paint has dried, children draw tiny heads, bodies and antennae on the fireflies.

• Draw a horizontal line across the middle of the jar.

• Fill in blanks on addition paper by counting the number of fireflies above the horizontal line and writing that number on the top line. Then count the number of fireflies below the horizontal line and write that number on the middle line. Add all the fireflies together and write the total on the bottom line.

F is for Fish

Ff

Before the Lesson

Prepare a sentence strip for each child. "My fish has _____ silver scales."

Show children how to use oil pastels by dabbing color onto paper, not rubbing it hard as is customary with crayons.

Have on Hand

9" x 12" white construction paper
oil pastels
aluminum foil cut into 3" squares
pencils

Read Aloud

Rainbow Fish by Marcus Pfister
Rainbow Fish to the Rescue
    by Marcus Pfister

Talk About

This is an excellent opportunity to talk about friendship and caring. Allow children to share about times they have asked others to play or times when they have felt left out.

Kids Create

- Use pencil to draw a fish on white construction paper.
- Color the fish with oil pastels and cut it out.
- Tear aluminum foil into scales and glue them on the fish.
- Count the scales and write the number in the sentence.
- Display the colored fish and sentence strips on the bulletin board.

My fish has 10 silver scales.

My fish has 12 silver scales.

F is for Frog

Ff

Before the Lesson

Trace the frog's head pattern on page 38 onto tagboard and cut it out for a pattern, one for each child.

Prepare a sentence strip for each child: "I'm a wide-mouthed frog, and I eat ___."

Show children how to make green paint by mixing yellow and blue paint.

Have on Hand

9" x 12" white construction paper
12" x 18" green construction paper
yellow and blue finger paint
red construction paper cut into 1" x 6"
    pieces
construction paper scraps in assorted colors
crayons

Read Aloud

The Wide Mouthed Frog by Keith Faulkner

Talk About

Write on the chalkboard *I'm a wide-mouthed frog, and I eat _____.* Have children pretend they are frogs and tell what they like to eat.

Kids Create

- Children mix yellow and blue paint and finger-paint the whole 9" x 12" sheet of construction paper.

- After the paint has dried, use a black crayon to trace the tagboard pattern of the frog's head on the painted paper and cut it out.

- Make construction paper eyes and glue them on.

- Make a tongue by curling a strip of red construction paper around a pencil and glue it down.

- Draw the body on green construction paper and cut it out.

- Glue the head and sentence strip onto the body and complete the sentence.

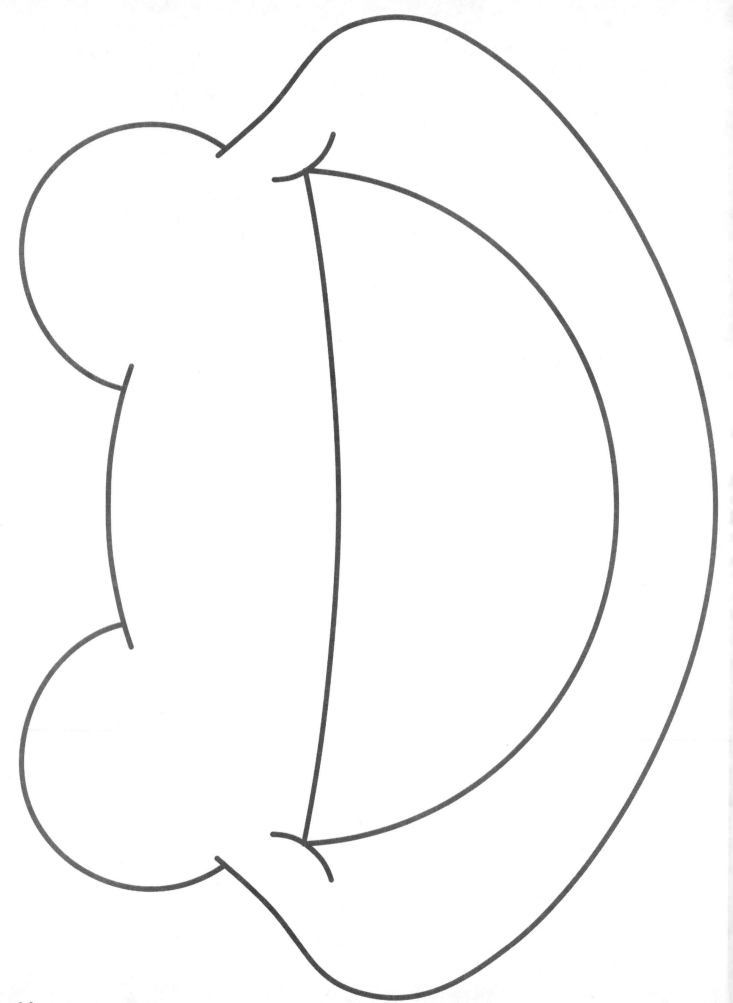

38

G is for **G**umball

Gg

Before the Lesson

Make a copy of the gumball machine on page 40 for each child.

Write each child's name with black marker on the gumball machine pattern.

Have on Hand

gumballs
copies of gumball machine pattern for
    each child
scraps of colored construction paper for
    gumballs
scissors
glue
black marker

Read Aloud

Gum on the Drum by Barbara Gregorich
    and Joan Hoffman

Talk About

Play a guessing game of What's in My Bag? Fill a brown paper bag with gumballs. Tell children you have a surprise in the bag and they need to guess what it is by asking "yes" and "no" questions, such as: Is it big? Is it soft? Record answers on the chalkboard. When the children have several good clues, allow them to guess what's in the bag.

Kids Create

• Cut out several round gumballs in a variety of colors and glue them on the top of the gumball machine.

• Children identify the beginning letter of the color words: Ask: What letter does *red* start with? Green? Blue? Yellow? Black? Pink? Purple? White? (If orange paper is used, children will need help with the beginning sound.)

• Children count the number of each color of gumballs in their gumball machines. Ask: How many red gumballs do you have? Green? Blue? Etc. Have children take turns telling how many gumballs they have in each color.

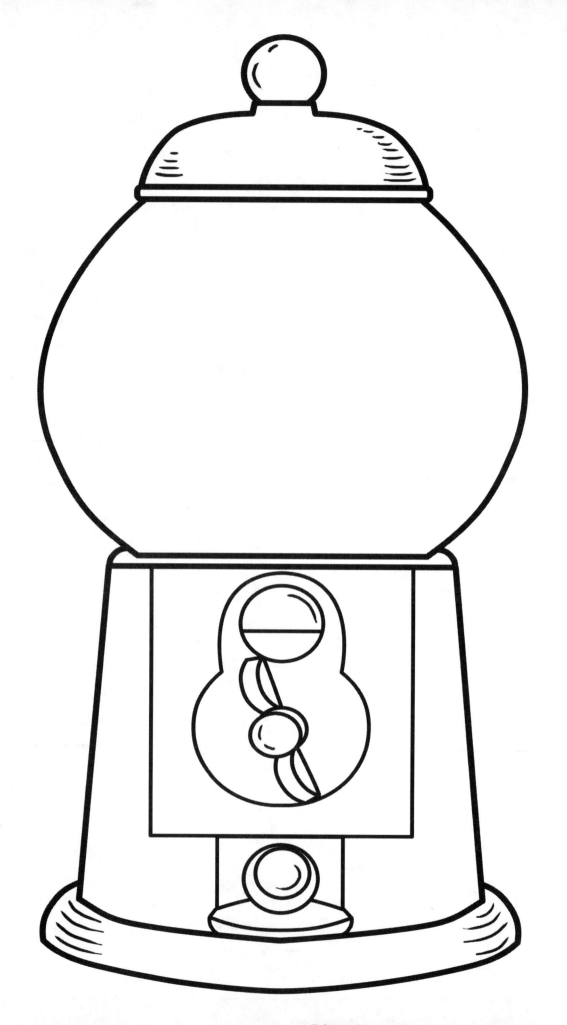

40

G is for Golden Goose

Gg

Before the Lesson

Write each child's name on a 3" x 5" card. Draw a large goose on tagboard (enlarge the illustration above) and cut it out. Spread glue over a portion of the goose and add feathers. Repeat until the goose is covered with feathers.

Spray-paint the goose gold.

Have on Hand

drawing paper
pencils
crayons
glue
scissors
1" x 4" white paper for each child
tagboard
feathers
gold spray paint

Read Aloud

The Golden Goose by Uri Schulevitz

Talk About

On chart paper write the repeating verse from the story:

Hokety, pokety, stickety, stuck,
Poor _____ was down on his (her) luck.
Wiggle and pull, he or (she) couldn't shake loose;
He (she) still had to stay with the simpleton's goose.

Review the verse with the children until they can say it with you. Pick one child's name at a time and have the child come up to the front. Use the child's name in the blank when repeating the rhyme. As the children are called in succession, have them "stick" to the person in front until all the children are "stuck" in a line.

Kids Create

• Children draw pictures of themselves and color and cut them out.

• They write their names on 1" x 4" paper.

Display the cut-out golden goose on the left of the bulletin board. Attach drawings of children close together in a line behind the goose. Staple each child's name under his or her drawing.

G is for **G**hosts on the **G**o

Gg

Before the Lesson

Cut ghost shapes out of white burlap or felt.

Prepare a sentence strip for each child. "My ghost likes to go _____."

Set up a sewing station where you, a parent or classroom aide can work with three to four students at a time.

Cover work tables with newspaper.

Have on Hand

1 8" x 12" piece of white burlap or felt for each child
assorted colors of felt cut into 3" x 4" pieces
assorted colors of yarn cut into 25" lengths, one per child
plastic sewing needles
construction paper
glue
scissors
crayons

Read Aloud

Ten Timid Ghosts by Jennifer O'Connell

Talk About

Have children work in small groups. Using the list below, assign children props to make for acting out the story. When they finish making the props, assign 10 children to be ghosts and one to be the witch. The rest of the children will help with the props as the teacher reads the story.

—skeleton   —owl
—bat   —ghoul
—cat   —spider
—vampire   —monster

Kids Create

- Children stitch around the edge of the burlap using running stitches indented about 3/4" in from the edge.

- Cut out pieces of colored felt and glue them in place to make a face on the ghost.

- Complete the sentence: "My ghost likes to go _____."

Before the Lesson

Draw a large, tall giraffe on yellow paper (enlarging the illustration above). Outline it with black marker and cut it out.

Display the giraffe on a classroom door or wall. Hang it low enough so children can reach it.

Cut random shapes from orange construction paper for Gerald the Giraffe's spots. Keep the spots handy in a box, with tape, on your desk or near the giraffe.

Have on Hand

large piece of yellow construction or
    butcher paper
orange construction paper
pencils
scissors
black marker
cellophane tape

Read Aloud

Giraffes Can't Dance by Giles Andreae

Talk About

Write the words *giraffe* and *Gerald* on the chalkboard. Explain that the words start with g but the sound is different than the g in *go, good, ghost, gumball, golden* and *goose*. Write other words that have a soft g sound: *George, gelatin, germ, general, generous, gentle, giant, gigantic* and *ginger*.

Ask about how Gerald felt when the animals were making fun of him. What happened later in the story that helped Gerald have the confidence to dance?

Have children talk about experiences when others have been nice to them. This is the focus of the lesson. Each time a child does a kind act, the receiving child will write that child's name on an orange spot and hang it on a large illustration of Gerald. The goal is to fill Gerald with spots.

Kids Create

- Children focus on being especially kind to each other.
- Children tell you when others in the class have been kind to them.
- Write the name of the child who was kind on an orange spot and glue it on Gerald the giraffe.

H is for
Hedgehog

Hh

Before the Lesson

Visit Jan Brett's web site:
www.janbrett.com

Click on the "Activities" section and under the letter C, go to "Character Masks."

Print a copy of the mask and duplicate one for each child.

Have on Hand

Crayola Model Magic™
white colored wooden toothpicks broken in half
watercolor paints

Read Aloud

The Hat by Jan Brett

Talk About

Ask the children who the main character of the story is. (Hedgie the Hedgehog) Review the story, paying special attention to the order of the animals. Divide children into small groups and give each group pictures of animals from the story, are available on Jan Brett's web site. Have each group work together to put the animals in the correct order.

Kids Create

- Make a hedgehog out of clay.
- Stick toothpicks into the body, broken side down, for spines.
- Allow it to dry thoroughly, then paint it.

H is for **H**eart

Hh

Before the Lesson

Draw a large heart on 8¹/₂" x 11" white paper and reproduce one for each child.

Make sentence strips and reproduce them on white paper.
"My heart is happy when _____."

Have on Hand

12" x 18" colored construction paper
glitter
heart-shaped pieces of foam
photo of each child

Read Aloud

The Boy Who Didn't Want to Be Sad
   by Rob Goldblatt

Talk About

Invite children to talk about things that make them happy and why.

Kids Create

- Color the heart and cut it out. Glue it on construction paper.
- Complete the sentence strip and glue it on the construction paper.
- Decorate the heart with crayons, foam hearts and glitter.

The teacher can glue each child's photo on the paper when the child has finished decorating it.

My heart is happy when
I'm eating ice cream.

y heart is happy when
I'm with my grandma.

Before the Lesson

Cover the tables that will be used for the art activity with newspaper or butcher paper.

Have on Hand

copies of the hippo face pattern on page 47
construction paper
buttons
sequins
feathers
craft foam
yarn
crayons
scissors
glue

Read Aloud

A Hippopotamus Ate the Teacher
  by Mike Thaler

Talk About

Discuss what makes a hippopotamus different from other animals. List physical characteristics on the chalkboard.

Kids Create

- Children color the hippo and cut it out.
- Cut yarn pieces and glue them on the hippo for hair.
- Make a construction paper hat and decorate it with craft items.
- Glue the hat on the hippo.
- Give the hippo a name beginning with H.

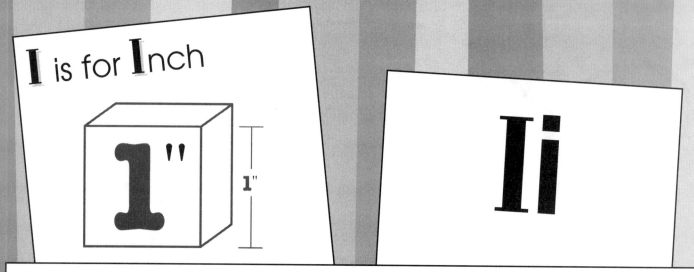

I is for Inch

Ii

Before the Lesson

Print a sentence strip onto 8½" x 11" paper and reproduce it for each child.
"The _____ is _____ inches long."

Have on Hand

8½" x 11" white paper
construction paper cut into 1" squares
magazines and catalogs with suitable
    items for children to cut out
scissors
glue
ruler and yardstick

Read Aloud

Inch by Inch by Leo Lionni

Talk About

Using a ruler, show children how long one inch is. Measure a few small flat items and write each measurement on the chalkboard next to the name of the item. Show children how you can get the same measurements using 1" paper squares. Select other classroom items and ask the children to estimate how many inches high or wide the items are. Measure with a ruler or yardstick for each actual height or width. Compare the estimates with the actual measurements.

Have children listen for the short i sound in *inch* and *insects*. What other words have the short i sound? (*instrument, if, imagine, inspect, it, itself, sit, did* and *him*) Write the words on the chalkboard as you say them so children can see the letter i.

Kids Create

- Each child looks through magazines or catalogs, cuts out a picture of one large item, person or animal, and glues it on paper with a measurement sentence.
- Lay out 1" squares to measure the height or width of the pictured item.
- Glue the squares in place to show measurement.
- Complete the sentence strip independently or with teacher assistance.

The __robot__ is __6__
inches long.

48

I is for **I**nsect

Ii

Before the Lesson

Set up a sewing station and cover a table with cloth or paper.

Have on Hand

9" x 12" pieces of burlap (burlap is available in most craft and fabric stores)
5" squares of felt
25" lengths of yarn, three per child
plastic sewing needles
permanent markers
scissors
glue

Read Aloud

Insects Are My Life by Megan McDonald
Know It Alls: Bugs by Christopher Nicholas

Talk About

Name the main physical characteristics of an insect: six legs, three body parts (head, thorax and abdomen) and a hard outer shell called an exoskeleton.

Sing

Sing this song to the tune of "B-I-N-G-O," to help children remember the physical characteristics of insects:

All insects have three body parts,
Six legs and exoskeleton.
Ex - o - skel - e - ton
Ex - o - skel - e - ton
Ex - o - skel - e - ton
Six legs, three body parts.

Kids Create

• Children each choose an insect that interests them and, with a permanent marker, draw it on a square of felt. (Remind children not to draw spiders as they have eight legs and are arachnids, not insects.)

• Cut out the insect and glue it on burlap. Decorate it with pieces of felt.

• Stitch the insect's path with yarn.

• Stitch a border with yarn. (This will require two lengths of yarn.)

I is for **I**ce Cream

Ii

Before the Lesson

Plan a field trip to the local scoop shop where children can learn more about ice cream.

Write the most common ice cream flavors on the chalkboard or chart paper for the children to use when completing the sentence.

Have on Hand

8$\frac{1}{2}$" x 11" white paper with sentence printed at the bottom: "I like _____ ice cream."
large sheet of graph paper
scissors
glue
brown construction paper for ice cream cones
5" squares of construction paper in ice cream colors

Read Aloud

From Cow to Ice Cream
   by Bertram T. Knight

Talk About

Invite children to talk about their favorite ice cream treat: cones, bars, cups or sundaes? What is each child's favorite flavor? Do a simple bar graphing activity of favorite flavors. Introduce the long i sound in *ice cream*. Name other words with the long i sound: *child, bicycle, Iowa, idea, find, Michael* and *pie*. Write them on the chalkboard for the children to see.

Kids Create

• Each child draws an ice cream cone on brown paper and cut it out.
• Draw three scoops of ice cream on colored paper and cut them out.
• Glue the cone and scoops on the white paper.
• They complete the sentence by writing their favorite flavors.

Invite parents to help plan a surprise ice cream treat!

J is for Jelly Beans

Yum! Jelly Beans

Jj

Before the Lesson

Print a number sentence at the bottom of white paper and reproduce it for each child.

_____ + _____ = _____

Fill plastic bags with 10 jelly beans each.

Have on Hand

8½" x 11" white paper
jelly beans, 10 assorted colors per child
small plastic bags
crayons
scissors
pencils
glue

Read Aloud

Jelly Beans and Gummy Things
by Lorraine Long and Mary Lou Roberts

Talk About

Review the j sound at the beginning of *jelly beans*. Give children jelly beans to sort by color. Show them how to make an addition sentence using two sets of jelly beans.

Kids Create

• Use the jelly beans to practice addition.

• On the white paper, above the number sentence, draw a figure with his hands up juggling.

• On a separate paper, draw 5 to 10 jelly beans and color each one.

• Cut out the jelly beans and glue them on the paper. Some of the 10 jelly beans should be on one side of the juggler and the rest on the other side of the juggler.

• Complete the number sentence by counting the number of jelly beans on each side and adding them together.

Before the Lesson

Make a sandwich booklet by placing two sheets of writing paper inside two sheets of tagboard, stapling them along the left side. (The tagboard is the bread.) Make one for each child.

Write *The Giant _____ Sandwich* on the cover.

Have on Hand

tagboard and writing paper cut into 9" squares
permanent black marker
pencils
crayons
stapler
long loaf of Italian or French bread
slicing bread knife
2-4 flavors of jam
plastic knives

Read Aloud

The Giant Jam Sandwich
    by John Vernon Lord and Janet Burroway

Talk About

Encourage children to talk about their favorite kinds of sandwiches. Invite them to create silly sandwiches, such as a chocolate sandwich or a flower sandwich. What flavors of jams can the children name? List them on the chalkboard.

Kids Create

• Color the edges of the book brown to look like bread crust.

• Choose a kind of sandwich and write it on the line on the cover.

• Draw sandwich filling on the inside pages.

• Share the finished sandwich books.

Make real, giant jam sandwiches with the class. Bring in a long loaf of French or Italian bread and two or three flavors of jam—grape, strawberry, cherry, blueberry. Slice the bread in half, then cut the loaf into slices for each child. Using plastic knives, the children can spread the jam on.

J is for Jamberry

Jj

Before the Lesson

Choose colored construction paper the color of jamberries and other berries—red, blue, purple.

Have on Hand

colored construction paper cut into 4" squares
9" x 12" white construction paper
pencils
crayons
scissors

Read Aloud

Jamberry by Bruce Degen

Talk About

Tell the children you are going to play a name game. You will say a child's name, but instead of it beginning with its correct letter, it will begin with J. When the name starts with a vowel, just add a J; don't drop the first letter. (Examples: Sarah—Jarah. Austin—Jaustin. Names that begin with J, like John or Justin, stay the same.) As you say each child's name, have him or her do an action beginning with J (*jump, jog* or *jiggle*). Next, tell the children they will be making a bulletin board where

they are covered in jamberries like the characters in the book.

Kids Create

- Draw pictures of themselves on white construction paper as tall as the paper.

- Cut out the drawings.

- They draw four to five jamberries on 4" squares of colored paper, print their "J" names on each jamberry and cut them out.

- Children help put up a bulletin board display of the drawings and "J" name jamberries.

Before the Lesson

Using white paper, cut out a diamond-shaped kite for each child and print a different hour at the bottom of each one. (Based on the times shown on page 55.)

Tape kites around the room at children's eye level.

Cut apart the clocks on page 55 and give one to each child.

Have on Hand

large teaching clock
yarn cut into 18" lengths for kite strings
3 pieces of 3" x 4" construction paper for
    each child
crayons
scissors
glue
clock templates on page 55

Read Aloud

Moonlight Kite by Helen E. Buckley

Talk About

Review telling time by the hour. Work with children to practice matching clocks to an hour you call out.

Kids Create

• Children walk around the room each with a paper clock looking for a kite with the same time.

• After the child matches the clock to a kite, he or she may have that kite to color.

• Glue the clock on the kite and attach a piece of yarn for the kite's string.

• Use three 3" x 4" pieces of colored construction paper to make bows for the kite's tail.

• Write the matching time on each bow.

K is for Kangaroo Rhymes

Kk

Before the Lesson

Pre-select 8 to 10 nursery rhymes to read aloud.

Have on Hand

writing paper
pencils
crayons

Read Aloud

Mother Goose by Sylvia Long
My Very First Mother Goose by Iona Opie

Talk About

After reading some well-known nursery rhymes, show children how to make up funny, kooky rhymes by substituting the word *kangaroo* for different items. Example: "Mary had a little kangaroo; it's fur was white as snow." "It's raining, it's pouring, the old kangaroo is snoring." Have children work in pairs to create their own rhymes to share with the class.

Kids Create

Working in pairs:

• Children dictate their kooky kangaroo rhymes and the teacher writes each one at the bottom of the writing paper.

• Illustrate the rhyme together.

• Share each rhyme with the class, then place the rhymes in a class book.

• Ask children which rhymes they thought were the funniest.

Before the Lesson

Make a sentence strip for each child. "Koala Lou can _____."

Make this headline for a bulletin board display: "Koala Lou, I DO love you!"

Have on Hand

9" x 12" white construction paper
pencils
crayons
scissors

Read Aloud

Koala Lou by Mem Fox

Talk About

Discuss all the things Koala Lou was able to do in the story. Review the repeating line, "Koala Lou, I DO love you!" Talk about how the mother always loved Koala Lou, even when Koala Lou didn't win the gum tree climbing event. Have the children list other activities they think Koala Lou would be good at. Have them draw pictures of Koala Lou doing the listed activities. Display the finished art on the bulletin board.

Kids Create

Working in pairs:

• Children draw a picture of Koala Lou, then cut it out. (Draw a step-by-step sample of a koala on the chalkboard so children have a visual to follow.)

• Complete the sentence strip and attach it to Koala Lou.

• Add children's koala drawings and sentences to the bulletin board.

This is an ideal time to talk about the native habitat of kangaroos and koalas—Australia, where author Mem Fox lives. Bring in library books showing kangaroos grazing and koalas in eucalyptus trees.

Koala Lou can read a book!

L is for Lunch Box

Ll

Before the Lesson

Fold 9" x 12" colored construction paper vertically for each child. Trace the lunch box pattern on each paper. (The fold should be at the top.) The lunch box will need to open from the bottom. Cut out the area in the handle so the children can hold the lunch box, page 59.

Have on Hand

copies of lunch box pattern on page 59
 traced on colored construction paper
copies of sentence starter: "I filled my
 lunch box with _____."
9" x 12" construction paper and scraps
stickers
crayons
glue
paper clips
3" x 1/2" strips of paper (two per lunch box)

Read Aloud

I Need a Lunchbox by Jeanette Caines
The Lunchbox Surprise
 by Grace Maccarone

Talk About

Ask children to tell what treats they would like to have packed in their lunch boxes.

Encourage each child to name something different than what the other children said.

Kids Create

• Have children cut out a lunch box.

• On the outside of the lunch box glue the sentence starter, "I filled my lunch box with _____."

• Decorate the outside of the lunch box with stickers and crayons.

• Use construction paper scraps to make items for inside the lunch box and glue them in place.

• Write words describing the items inside the lunch box to complete the sentence starter.

• Show the lunch box to the rest of the class.

L is for Letter and Love

Ll

Before the Lesson

Write each child's address on an envelope.

Write *love* on the chalkboard; write it in all caps, all lowercase and with a capital L: *LOVE, love, Love.*

Have on Hand

1 blank letter from page 61 for each child
colored pencils
envelopes

Read Aloud

A Letter to Amy by Ezra Jack Keats

Talk About

Provide readiness for children who will be writing letters to people who live in their homes. In the letter each child will tell about different activities he or she does at school. Encourage children to share some ideas they will include in their letters.

Kids Create

- This is a good activity to do while children are at centers in the classroom. You will need to work with each child individually.

- With your help, children complete the letter form. Encourage them to write as much as they can on their own.

- Decorate the letter using colored pencils.

- Review each child's address with him or her before putting the letter in the envelope.

- Depending on your class size, decide if you want to mail the letters home or if you want the children to hand deliver them. If mailing them, take a class trip to the post office.

L is for Letter and Love

Dear _____ ,

I _____ you!

At school I like _____ .

At home I like _____ .

 Love,

_____

L is for Letter and Love

Dear _____ ,

I _____ you!

At school I like _____ .

At home I like _____ .

Love,

_____

L is for **L**izard

Ll

Before the Lesson

Tape four pieces of sandpaper on a table, leaving enough space between them for children to work.

Tape the lizard pattern, page 63, on top of the sandpaper to prevent it from moving as the children make lizard rubbings. Demonstrate how to color the lizard while it is taped to the sandpaper. Kids will be amazed at the texture created by the sandpaper!

Have on Hand

copies of lizard pattern on page 63
sandpaper
9" x 12" construction paper
crayons
glue

Read Aloud

Amazing Lizards by Fay Robinson

Talk About

Review facts about lizards from the book. Have each child tell one fact he or she learned about lizards.

Kids Create

- Each child creates a lizard rubbing.
- Children cut out their lizards and glue them on construction paper.
- Draw a habitat around the lizard.
- Dictate one lizard fact to the teacher to write on the paper.

Lizards can change their color.

Before the Lesson

Reproduce the three sentences under "Talk About" for each child.

Have on Hand

12" x 18" construction paper
paint
pencils

Read Aloud

Go Away Big Green Monster
   by Ed Emberley
We Are Monsters by Mary Packard

Talk About

Look at and discuss the various physical characteristics of the monsters in the two books. Read the following incomplete sentences to children and have them think about how they would complete them.

My name is _____.
I am a monster who lives _____.
I eat _____ and drink _____.

Tell children they will be using their imaginations to paint pictures of monsters.

Kids Create

- Children paint pictures of monsters from their imagination.
- Complete three sentences about the monsters with teacher assistance.

M is for
Magnificent
Monster
Munchies

Mm

Before the Lesson

Place six assorted, colored m & m's™ and six mini marshmallows in a small plastic bag for each child.

Have on Hand

copy of "My Monster Munchy" on page 66 for each child
electric griddle
pancake mix and ingredients listed
6 m & m's™ and 6 mini marshmallows for each child
small plastic bags
plastic plates (pancakes will stick to paper plates)
colored pencils

Read Aloud

Monster Math by Anne Miranda

Talk About

Tell children they're in for a treat! They'll be using m & m's™ and mini marshmallows to create monster faces on pancakes. However, before making the faces they need to make plans on paper. Show them how to draw a pancake on the paper, then draw where they will place their m & m's™ and marshmallows, six of each (m & m's™ should be shown in color; marshmallows may be pencil outlines).

Kids Create

- Children plan their monster faces by drawing them on planning pages. They complete the number sentences below the drawing.

- After the pancakes are made, children use m & m's™ and mini marshmallows as drawn on their planning pages to make magnificent monster munchies.

- Children show their monster faces before enjoying the pancakes.

My Monster Munchy

____ m & m's™

\+ ____ marshmallows

\= ____ munchies

M is for Mud

Mm

Before the Lesson

Use permanent markers to write each child's name on the bottom of an aluminum pan.

Set up a brick-making area in class or, depending on the season and weather, do the activity outdoors.

Have each child bring an old shirt to wear for this messy activity.

Have on Hand

large plastic tub for mixing
water
soil
sand
dry grass
2" x 5" aluminum pan for each child
permanent markers

Read Aloud

Mud Puddle by Robert Munsch

Talk About

Ask the children how they think mud is made. How does mud feel? What can mud be used for? Explain that mud can be made into bricks by mixing it with sand, water and grass, then letting it dry. These are called adobe bricks and are used to make houses in some places.

Kids Create

Working with three to four children at a time, have them:

• Pour dirt, sand, grass and water into the plastic tub.

• Mix it with their hands.

• Use their hands to fill their aluminum pans with the mud mixture.

Allow the bricks to air dry for two to three days, then pop them out of the tins to finish drying. Have children work in small groups to practice building a structure with their bricks. Send a brick home with each child in a plastic zip-type bag.

N is for Nails

Nn

Before the Lesson

Cut wood into 6" x 6" blocks. Sand the edges of the wooden blocks.

Cut yarn in 32" lengths, four per child.

Have on Hand

6" x 6" blocks of wood
nails
hammers
markers
yarn in a variety of colors

Read Aloud

Tools by Gallimard Jeunesse and
    Claude Delafosse

Talk About

Have children talk about hand and power tools their parents use at home or at work. Bring in simple hand tools—screwdriver, hammer, pliers, wrench—and discuss how each is used.

Kids Create

Working in groups of three or four:

- Children decorate the block of wood with markers.

- Hammer eight nails into one side of the block. (The nails should be spread out on the 6" x 6" block and hammered in firmly.)

- Wrap yarn around the nails to create a colorful design. Children may need help attaching the strands of yarn.

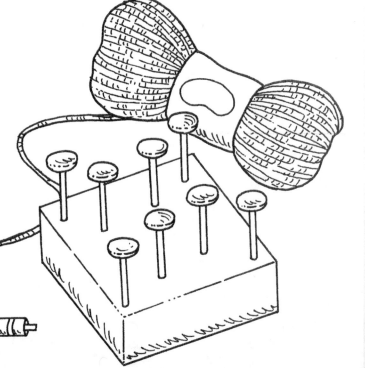

Before the Lesson

Glue each child's photo in the center of a 9" x 12" piece of red construction paper.

Cover the work table with plastic or newspaper.

Have on Hand

photo of each child
9" x 12" red, white and blue construction paper
patriotic rubber stamps; red and blue stamp pads
silver and gold metallic markers
glue
scissors with decorative cutting edges

Read Aloud

A Is for America by David Scillian
Celebrate the 50 States by Loreen Leedy

Talk About

Introduce children to the 50 states and Washington, D.C. Using a large map of the United States, allow the children to share places they have been or know about. Point out your state. Discuss what it means to be a nation.

Kids Create

- Using scissors with decorative edges, children cut around the edges of the red paper.
- Glue the red paper on the center of the blue construction paper.
- Using rubber stamps and ink pads, stamp patriotic shapes onto white construction paper and cut out around them.
- Glue the stamped shapes onto the blue construction paper.
- Decorate the page with gold and silver markers.

Before the Lesson

Place a pile of craft sticks at each table.

Make a sentence strip for each child. "There are _____ animals in Noah's Ark."

Have on Hand

12" x 18" light blue construction paper
10-12 craft sticks per child
craft foam animals (available in craft stores or craft sections of super stores)
crayons
glue

Read Aloud

Two by Two by Barbara Reid

Talk About

Review the story, asking the children to recall the different animals that entered the ark. This is an appropriate time to do some creative drama as children act out the parts of animals and practice counting by twos. Discuss the shape of an ark.

Kids Create

- Children count out 10-12 sticks and place them on blue construction paper.
- Show children how to lay out the sticks to form an outline of an ark.
- Glue each stick in place.
- Draw windows and a door in the ark and color it.
- Glue pairs of foam animals onto the ark and add background details such as a sun and a rainbow.
- Count the number of animals and complete the sentence strip. Glue it below the ark.

There are _8_ animals in Noah's Ark.

O is for Owl

Oo

Before the Lesson

Cut brown construction paper into 6" x 9" pieces for the owl's body and 6" x 6" pieces for the head.

Have on Hand

12" x 18" brown construction paper
yellow and orange construction paper scraps
black crayons
large construction paper tree with several branches on a bulletin board

Read Aloud

Owl Moon by Jane Yolen

Talk About

After reviewing the story, have students tell about times they have heard or seen owls. Let children imitate the sound an owl makes.

Kids Create

- Draw a large circle for the owl's head on the smaller piece of paper and cut it out.
- Draw an oval for the body on the larger piece of paper and cut it out.

- Glue the head to the top of the body.
- Use yellow and orange scraps to make eyes and a beak and glue them on.
- Draw legs and talons.
- Add wings, feathers and ear tuft details with black crayon.
- Make a branch and put a few leaves on each side.
- Count the number of leaves on each side and write the addition problem.

$2 + 3 = 5$

O is for Octopus

Oo

Before the Lesson

Fill the squirt bottle with water.

Pour Kool-Aid™ powder into the cupcake papers.

Cut off the curved edge of the coffee filters along one edge so the edge is straight. The other edge should remain curved.

Cut construction paper into 2" x 5" strips.

Cover the tables with newspaper.

Have on Hand

chart paper
markers
coffee filters, one for each child
construction paper in assorted colors
Kool-Aid™, several flavors in different
    colors
squirt bottle
glue
scissors
paper cupcake holders

Read Aloud

An Octopus Is Amazing by Patricia Lauber

Talk About

Review the facts mentioned in the story and list them on chart paper to display with the finished octopuses. Listen for the short o sound in *octopus*. Name other words beginning with the short o sound: *October, otter, ostrich, on, opposite.*

Kids Create

- Squirt the coffee filter with water until it is damp.

- Sprinkle different colors of Kool-Aid™ onto the coffee filter.

- Spray the filter again to blend colors, then allow it to dry.

- After the filter is dry, choose eight strips of construction paper for legs. Cut wavy shapes along the sides and round off the edges of each strip so the legs look soft and rubbery.

- Glue the legs on the curved edge of the filter.

- Make eyes from scraps of construction paper and glue them on.

O is for Otter

Oo

Before the Lesson

Write a different number word at the bottom of the otter pattern on page 74 for each child.

Cut brown or gray construction paper into 3" x 5" strips, four per child.

Have on Hand

copy of otter pattern on page 74 for each child
12" x 18" brown or gray construction paper
scraps of construction paper for shell and rock
crayons
scissors
glue

Read Aloud

Swim the Silver Sea, Joshie Otter
by Nancy White Carlstrom
Otter on His Own: The Story of a Sea Otter
by Doe Boyle

Talk About

After reading *Swim the Silver Sea, Joshie Otter*, help children retell the story in sequence. Talk about the different Arctic animals that Joshie Otter saw on his journey. Can the children recall how an otter gets food out of a shell? Review number words one to ten and the sound of short o as in *otter, octopus, October, ostrich, on* and *opposite*.

Kids Create

- Color the otter pattern and cut it out.
- For paws and legs, round off the bottom of the four strips and draw lines on them for toes. Glue them in place on the body.
- Draw a rock on the otter's stomach.
- On the shell or rock, write the number that matches the number word.

74

O is for Ocean

Oo

Before the Lesson

Cover the art tables and set up art supplies.

Cover the bulletin board with blue paper.

Have on Hand

chart paper
large piece of blue bulletin board paper
    for ocean mural
construction paper
foam
felt
watercolor paints
sequins
tissue paper
markers
tape
glue
stapler

Read Aloud

Somewhere in the Ocean
    by Jennifer Ward and T.J. Marsh
    (Look for the hidden number on each
    page.)
Out of the Ocean by Debra Frasier

Talk About

Share some of the interesting new facts learned about the ocean and ocean animals. Encourage children to share other information they know about the ocean. Write the information on chart paper, make sure it is accurate. Listen for the sound of the long o in *ocean*. Have children name other words with a long o sound and write them on the chalkboard or chart paper: *over, only, obey, oats, open, boat, fold* and *soap*.

Kids Create

• Children select an ocean animal to create.

• Make an animal out of paper, craft foam or felt.

• Decorate the animal with assorted art supplies.

• Attach the ocean animal to the blue ocean mural. As children finish, they may add details such as coral and seaweed to the blue bulletin board background.

Hang the chart paper with ocean facts next to the mural.

P is for Popcorn

Pp

Before the Lesson

Go to www.popcorn.org for an array of printable popcorn coloring pages and teaching ideas.

Prepare an area of the room for popping corn. Before popping corn, show children unpopped corn in a one-cup measuring cup. Ask each child to estimate how many cups of popped popcorn it will make. Write the children's estimates on the chalkboard or chart paper. After popping the corn, have children count how many cups of popcorn there are. Who came the closest to correct amount?

Have on Hand

package of popping corn
electric fry pan with lid
1 cup measuring cup
napkins or paper plates
chart paper
oil
salt

Read Aloud

The Popcorn Shop by Alice Low
Popcorn by Frank Asch
The Popcorn Book by Tomie dePaola

Talk About

Ask children when they usually have popcorn. Is it when they go to see a movie or do they have popcorn at home, too? Invite them to tell how they like their popcorn—plain, with melted butter, dipped in melted caramel or another way.

Kids Create

• After the corn has popped and children have enjoyed the treat, have them retell the steps to follow in order, from setting up the popping area to eating the popped corn. On chart paper, write *We Made Popcorn.* Write each step as children dictate.

P is for **P**aper

Pizza

Pp

Before the Lesson

Cut brown, green, tan and red construction paper into 1¹/₂" squares.

Cut yellow paper into 1" x 3" strips.

Have on Hand

9" x 12" white construction paper, one
   sheet per child
brown, green, red, tan and yellow
   construction paper for toppings
scissors
glue
crayons
1 copy of pizza ingredients from page 78
   for each child

Read Aloud

Huggly's Pizza by Tedd Arnold
Pizza by Saturnino Romay

Talk About

Have children talk about their favorite pizza toppings. How many like their pizza with only sauce and cheese? Who likes sausage? Pepperoni? Mushrooms? Pineapple and ham?

Go to www.charlottediamond.com and click on the "music" carrot. On her CD, *10 Carrot Diamond*, listen to the song "I Am a Pizza." Copy the lyrics and teach the song to the class.

Sing these words to the tune of "B-I-N-G-O":

   There is a treat we like to eat,
   And pizza is its name O,
   P-I-Z-Z-A,
   P-I-Z-Z-A,
   P-I-Z-Z-A
   And pizza is its name O.

Kids Create

• Draw a whole pizza or a slice on white construction paper.

• Color the crust brown and the center red.

• Cut out sausage, pepperoni, mushrooms and green peppers from the 1¹/₂" squares and glue them on the pizza.

• Cut yellow paper into strips for cheese and glue them on the pizza.

• Count how many of each ingredient there are. Fill in the pizza ingredients on the page with the correct number.

Chef _____

My pizza has:

_____ pieces of sausage.

_____ pieces of mushroom.

_____ pieces of pepperoni.

_____ pieces of green pepper.

- -

Chef _____

My pizza has:

_____ pieces of sausage.

_____ pieces of mushroom.

_____ pieces of pepperoni.

_____ pieces of green pepper.

P is for **P**igs with **P**ockets

Pp

Before the Lesson

Reproduce the two-page pig pattern on pages 80-81 onto tagboard. Attach the two pages together to make a pig. Trace it on pink paper for each child.

Create a sentence strip and reproduce it for each child.
"My pig has _____ in its pocket."

Have on Hand

11" x 17" pink construction paper
tagboard
various fabrics cut into 3" x 4" pieces
two-part pig pattern on pages 80-81
   traced on pink construction paper for
   each child
crayons
scissors
glue
magazines and catalogs

Read Aloud

Pigs Aplenty, Pigs Galore!
   by David McPhail
Peter's Pocket by Judi Barrett

Talk About

Tell children they will be making "pigs with pockets." To reinforce the sound of the letter P, have them name items that begin with P that they might put in a pocket: pennies, purple or pink crayon, popcorn, peanuts.

Kids Create

• Color the pig, draw a face and draw clothes on it.

• With assistance, children apply glue along the bottom and two sides of a piece of fabric—making sure that the top of the pocket is open. They glue the pocket on the pig's jeans.

• Cut out an item that begins with P.

• When the glue is dry and the pocket is secure, put P items in it.

• Complete the sentence strip and attach it to the pig.

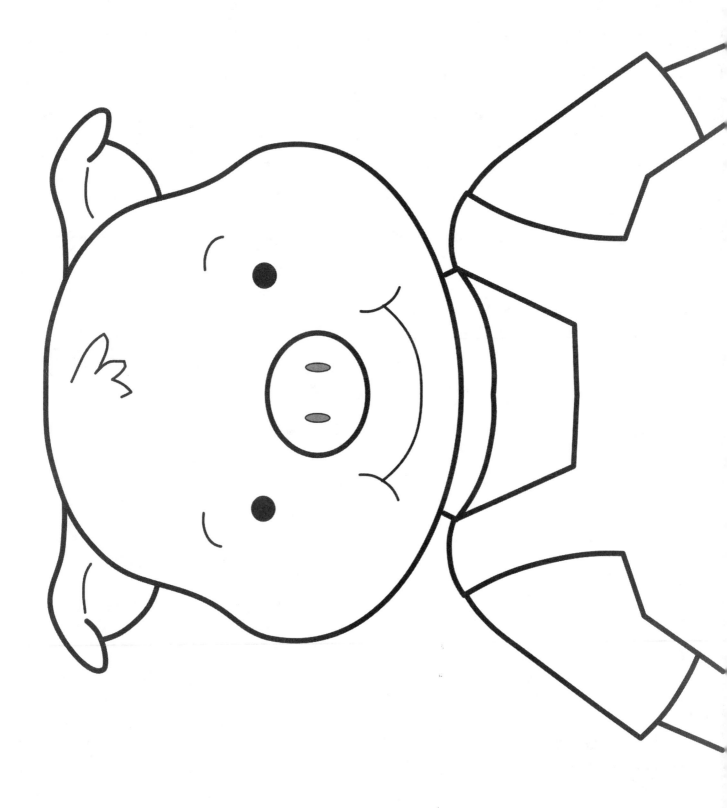

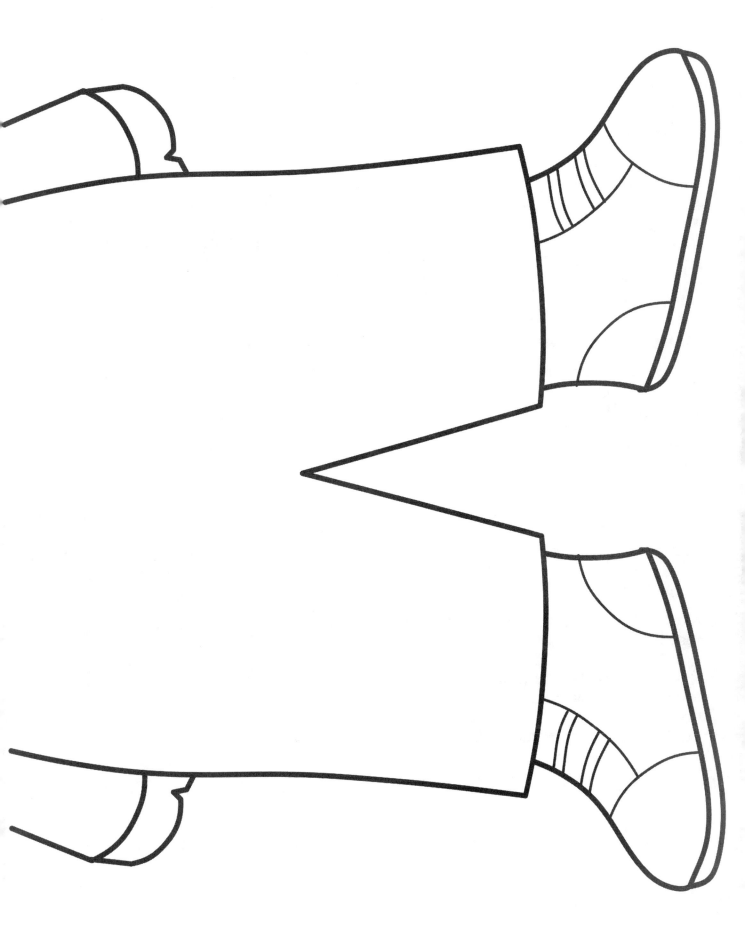

Before the Lesson

Cut construction paper into 2" x 18" strips.

Have on Hand

chart paper
colored markers
12" x 18" white construction paper

Read Aloud

Are There Any Questions? by Denys Cazet

Talk About

Ask children, "What is a question?" After they give their definitions, tell them that a question is a sentence calling for an answer: What time is it? What is your favorite color? Where do you live? Do you have a puppy? Invite them to each ask a question. Help them to hear the "Q" sound, which sounds like K (or C) together with W. List some common words beginning with Q on the chalkboard: *question, quilt, queen, quart, quiet, quit, quick, quack, quarter* and *quarrel.*

Kids Create

• Using different colors of markers, as each child asks a question write it on a sentence strip. Tack all the questions to a bulletin board. Read the questions aloud, letting a different child answer each one.

• Play The Question Game. Seat children in a circle. One child asks the child to his or her left a question. That child answers the question, then asks the child to his or her left a question. Continue until all the children have had a chance to ask a question and give an answer. Encourage them not to repeat a question someone else has asked.

Before the Lesson

Attach large coins from pages 84-85 to colored construction paper and display them for students to use as a reference. Use the colors: penny/green, nickel/pink, dime/purple, quarter/orange

Have on Hand

copies of quilt squares with coins on pages 84-85
oil pastels or crayons
large illustrations of coins—penny, nickel, dime, quarter
pink, purple, green and orange construction paper
scissors

Read Aloud

The Quilt Story by Tony Johnston

Talk About

Discuss the colors and patterns in quilts. Explain that a quilt is made by stitching together many different pieces of fabric to create a design, cutting a large piece of fabric for the bottom then sewing the top and bottom together with a soft filling in the middle. Many quilts are called patchwork quilts because they are made of many squares/patches sewn together. If possible, show children a patchwork quilt.

Review the names of coins. Which coin starts with the letter Q?

Kids Create

• Each child receives a paper showing four different coins. This set of four coins is one quilt square. They color each square according to the samples shown.

• Color coins brown for copper and gray for nickel and silver.

• Cut out each quilt square.

• Arrange them in a quilt on the bulletin board.

Q is for Queen

Qq

Before the Lesson

Cover the tables in the art area.

Have on Hand

1 strip of 1½" x 18" tagboard headband
    for each child
3 tagboard 1" triangles for each child
red, blue, green construction paper
gold glitter
gold or yellow paint
scissors
glue

Read Aloud

The Recess Queen by Alexis O'Neill
Queen of Hearts by Mary Engelbreit
Queen of the Class by Mary Engelbreit

Talk About

Ask children to share their thoughts on what a queen is (the wife of a king or a female sovereign of a country). Write their ideas on chart paper to get a general idea of how they view the role of a queen. Discuss ceremonial clothing worn by a queen at official functions (long robe and crown).

Why was Mean Jean referred to as a queen? Did she think she was better or more important than the other boys and girls?

Kids Create

• Children glue three triangles to the top center of the crown headband.

• Paint one side of the crown and triangles with gold or yellow paint. Sprinkle on gold glitter and allow it to dry.

• Cut construction paper into small circles and squares and glue them on the headband for jewels.

• Adjust each crown to fit the child's head.

R is for Rocket

Rr

Before the Lesson

Create a sentence starter and reproduce it for each child. Provide three lines for the children to write on.
"I _____ in my rocket."

Cut apart alphabet stickers and set them out on a table.

Have on Hand

11" x 17" white construction paper
colored construction paper
alphabet stickers
photo of each child
crayons
scissors
glue
red, orange and yellow tissue paper

Read Aloud

Boom! Zoom! by Judith Bauer Stamper
Space Race by Judith Bauer Stamper

Talk About

Tell children to close their eyes and imagine they are taking off from Earth, flying in a rocket. What do they see during their flight?

Kids Create

- Children make rockets with construction paper.

- They add windows and details with paper scraps and crayons, then glue their photos in the rocket windows.

- They find their name initials at the sticker table and place them on the rockets.

- Cut red and orange flames from tissue paper and glue them to the bottom of the rockets.

- Glue the rockets on backgrounds of construction paper.

- Draw what they imagine they are seeing on the background, then complete the sentence starter.

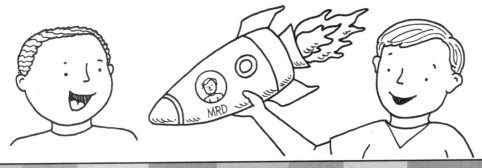

R is for Robot

Rr

Before the Lesson

Tear aluminum foil into pieces large enough to cover the cardboard pieces.

Create a sentence strip and reproduce it for each child.
"My robot can _____."

Have on Hand

5" x 6" cardboard, one per child
aluminum foil
construction paper
permanent markers
glue
clear tape

Read Aloud

Sammy and the Robots by Ian Whybrow

Talk About

Review the story and talk about some of the things Sammy and his robot did. Ask: "If you had a robot, what would you want it to do?" Have the children think of answers but not share them with anyone. Show the sample robot. When the children have completed their robots, they can tell what their robots can do.

Kids Create

- Cover the front cardboard with aluminum foil; turn the foil under and tape it to the back for the robot's body.

- Make a head from construction paper and tape it on the body. (Glue will not stick to the foil.)

- Draw buttons and gadgets on the body with permanent markers.

- Make arms and legs from paper scraps and tape them to the body.

- Finish the sentence to tell what the robot can do. Glue the sentence on the robot.

My robot can
clean my room

R is for Reindeer

Rr

Before the Lesson

Counting by 10s, create number cards for the children, one number on each 3" x 5" card.

Have on Hand

9" x 12" and 9" x 9" brown construction paper
4" x 4" yellow and white construction paper
construction paper scraps
crayons
scissors
glue
black marker
red pom-poms or crushed red tissue paper, one per child
blank 3" x 5" cards

Read Aloud

The Wild Christmas Reindeer by Jan Brett

Talk About

Ask the children to describe the physical characteristics of reindeer. Draw an oval on the chalkboard. As the children name parts of the reindeer, add them to your drawing. This will help children as they draw their own reindeer.

Practice counting by 10s. Pass out a 10s number card to each child. After the children have completed their reindeer, they will write the 10s number shown on the card on the reindeer's body. After everyone is finished, the children will put their reindeer in sequential order and practice counting by 10s.

Kids Create

• Children draw an oval on 9" x 12" brown paper for body and cut it out.

• Draw another oval on the smaller brown paper for the head and cut it out.

• Glue the head onto the body.

• Draw antlers on yellow paper, cut them out and glue them on the head.

• Glue a red pom-pom or crushed red tissue paper on for the nose and draw a mouth.

• Use paper scraps to make the legs and tail and glue them on.

• Write the number on the card on 4" x 4" white paper, cut it out and glue it on the reindeer.

After children put their deer in numerical order and count aloud by 10s, display the reindeer on the wall as a reference for counting by 10s.

S is for Star

Ss

Before the Lesson

Set up a glitter art table.

Have on Hand

9" x 12" construction paper in assorted colors
copies of star pattern on page 91 on
    yellow construction paper
crayons
scissors
glue
glitter
copies of the "I wish" sentences on page
    92, one for each child

Read Aloud

Lauras's Star by Klaus Baumgart
Laura's Christmas Star by Klaus Baumgart

Talk About

Recite the poem "Star Light, Star Bright"
with the children. Have each child tell
what he or she wishes for. Encourage the
children to think of others as they make
their wishes.

Kids Create

- Children color and decorate copies of
  the star.
- Complete the wish sentence, adding
  their names.
- Glue the star and sentence on
  background construction paper.
- Spread glitter on the star and paper.

90

_____'s Wish

I wish _____

_____ .

_____'s Wish

I wish _____

_____ .

S is for **S**nowflake

Ss

Before the Lesson

Create a sentence strip and reproduce it for each child.
"If I were a snowflake, I _____."

Set up a glitter area.

Have on Hand

coffee filters, one per child plus extras
photo of each child
9" x 12" construction paper
crayons
scissors
glue
glitter

Read Aloud

Geraldine's Big Snow by Holly Keller
The Snowy Day by Ezra Jack Keats
Snowballs by Lois Ehlert

Talk About

In an open area have children pretend they are snowflakes floating down. Encourage creative movement. Ask where they would like to land.

Kids Create

• Work with children in small groups to show them how to make a snowflake. Let them practice on white paper before cutting the filters.

• Children glue the snowflakes on the lower part of the construction paper.

• Complete the sentence and glue it to the top of the paper.

• Spread glue on the snowflake and decorate it with glitter.

• Glue the photo in the center of the snowflake.

If I were a snowflake, I would land on a monkey at the zoo.

S is for Seal

Ss

Before the Lesson

Create a sample as shown below as a guide.

Review how to write an addition number sentence: one numeral + another = total.

Have on Hand

copies of seal patterns on page 95, one per child
9" x 12" construction paper
craft foam shapes
crayons
scissors
glue

Read Aloud

Sammy the Seal by Syd Hoff

Talk About

How are seals different than other animals? What sounds do they make? How do they move? Show children your sample and tell them they will be making addition sentences with seals and shapes.

Kids Create

- Children color seals and cut them out.
- Glue the seals facing each other on the construction paper.
- Glue foam shapes (or shapes cut from construction paper) as if the seals are balancing them on their noses.
- Count the number of shapes above each seal's nose. Write an addition sentence about the shapes.
- Write the letter S and the word *seal* on the paper.

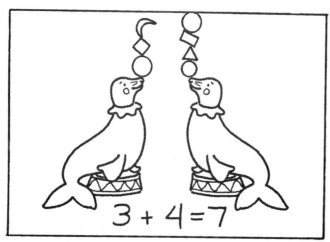

3 + 4 = 7

T is for Turtle

Tt

Before the Lesson

Create a sentence strip and reproduce it for each child.
"My turtle's name is _____."

Have on Hand

9" x 12" white construction paper
green construction paper cut into 2" x 5" strips; five per child
oil pastels or crayons
hair spray
scissors
glue

Read Aloud

Box Turtle at Long Pond
by William T. George
Turtle Splash! Countdown at the Pond
by Cathryn Falwell

Talk About

Ask children to talk about places where they have seen turtles.

My turtle's name is Timmy.

Sing

To the tune of "The Ants Go Marching":

Twisting Turtles

The turtles are twisting round and round,
Hurrah! Hurrah!

The turtles are twisting round and round,
Hurrah! Hurrah!

The turtles are twisting round and round.

Names beginning with T sit on the ground,

And we'll all go marching,

Till we all sit on the ground.

Continue the song and change the beginning sound until every child is sitting.

Kids Create

• Draw a turtle shell on white paper, color it with oil pastels and bring it to the teacher to be sprayed with hair spray. (This will keep the pastels from smearing.) Or color the shell with crayons.

• Draw four legs and a head on the green paper strips, cut them out and glue them to the body.

• Draw a face on the head.

• Give the turtle a name that starts with T. Print the name in the sentence strip and glue it below the turtle.

T is for Tiger

Tt

Before the Lesson

Reproduce a copy of the tiger head on page 98 at the top of a 12" x 18" sheet of orange construction paper for each child.

Have on Hand

copy of tiger head on page 98 on orange construction paper for each child
copy of one tie on page 99 on white paper for each child
12" x 18" orange construction paper
crayons
scissors
glue
black markers
craft foam shapes

Read Aloud

Sam and the Tigers
  by Julius Lester and Rachel Isadora
Tigress by Nick Dowson

Talk About

Have children name the different "big cats"—leopard, jaguar, tiger, lion. Ask how the tiger's appearance is different from the other big cats.

Kids Create

• Draw the tiger's body under its head on the orange paper and cut the tiger out.

• Draw stripes on the face and body with black crayon or marker.

• Decorate the tie by gluing a pattern on it with foam shapes.

• Glue the tie on the tiger.

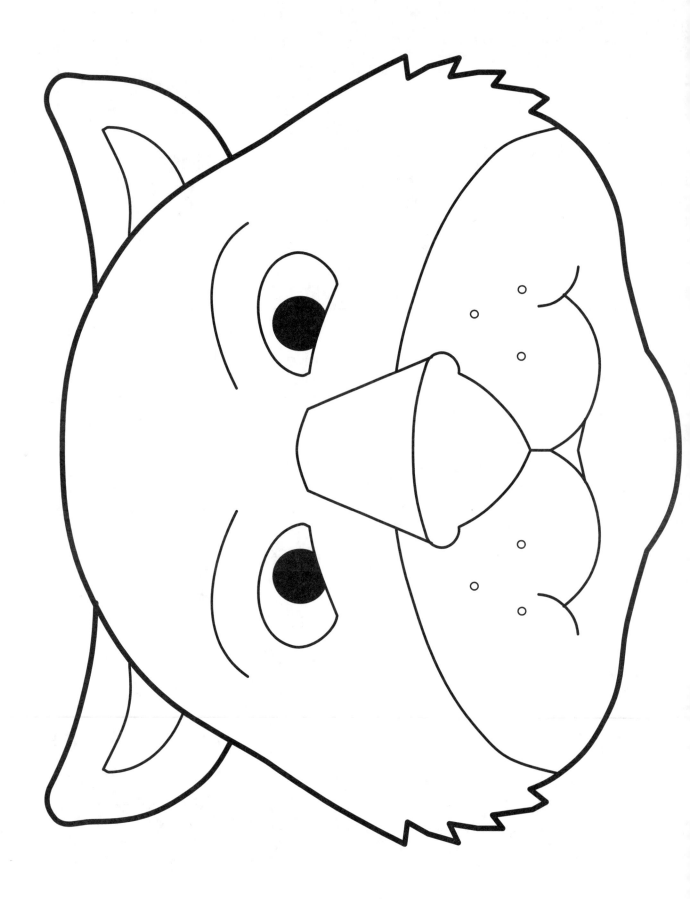

98

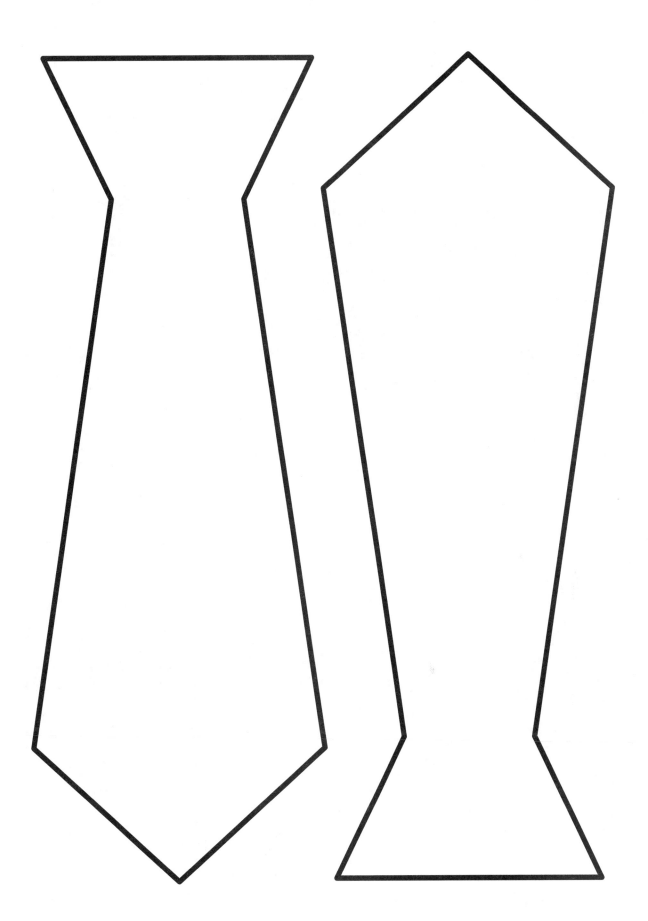

T is for **T**riangle
Turkey

Tt

Before the Lesson

Create a sentence strip and reproduce it for each child.
"My turkey has _____ feathers."

Set up an area for painting.

Make a sample turkey as shown below.

Have on Hand

5" wooden triangles
2" x 5" construction paper strips in assorted
    colors
3" x 6" brown construction paper
crayons
scissors
glue
brown paint

Read Aloud

Gracias the Thanksgiving Turkey
    by Joy Cowley

Talk About

Before reading the story, make a graph based on the question, "Do you think Gracias is a good name for a turkey?" Have "yes" and "no" columns where children write their names. After reading the story, review the graph and see if any of the children want to change their answers.

Kids Create

• Children paint their wooden triangles brown.

• Help children draw a head and neck on brown construction paper and cut them out. Draw a face on the head. Glue the head and neck on the front of the triangle.

• Make feathers from colored paper strips and glue them to the back of the triangle.

• Count the feathers and write the number in the sentence strip. Glue it to the bottom of the triangle.

• Set up a colorful display of finished turkeys.

U is for **U**p

Uu

Before the Lesson

Make tagboard patterns from pages 102-103.

Have on Hand

tagboard copy of the balloon on page 102, one per child

several copies of the basket on page 103 on tagboard for children to trace onto construction paper (cut on dotted line to make two baskets)

sight word cards

9" x 12" tagboard

6" x 9" construction paper

markers

scissors

yarn cut into 12" lengths, two per child

Read Aloud

Up, Up, Down by Robert Munsch

Talk About

Have children listen to the short u sound in the word *up*. Say other words with the short u sound and write them on the chalkboard: *uncle, under, until, umbrella, hungry, rug* and *sun*.

Tell children they will be making something that goes up. Give clues to see if they can guess what it is. Review sight words: give each child a sight word card and have him or her read it to you. Children will be writing their sight words on their hot air balloons.

Kids Create

• Children print their sight words in the middle of their balloons.

• Color the balloon with markers (remind the children not to color over the word).

• Cut out the balloon.

• They trace baskets on construction paper, write their names on them, decorate them and cut them out.

• Bring the balloon and basket to the teacher to have holes punched and string tied to connect them.

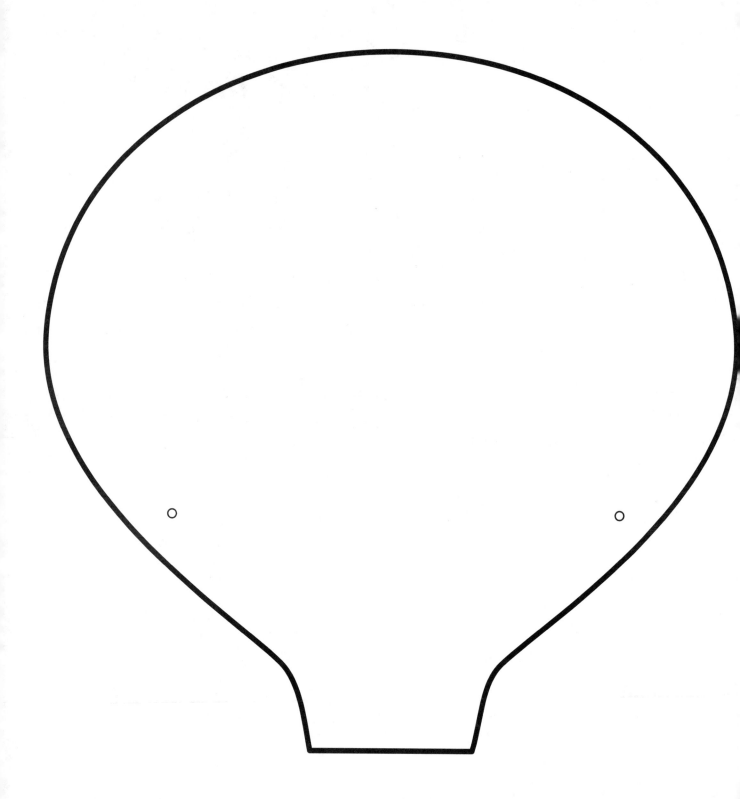

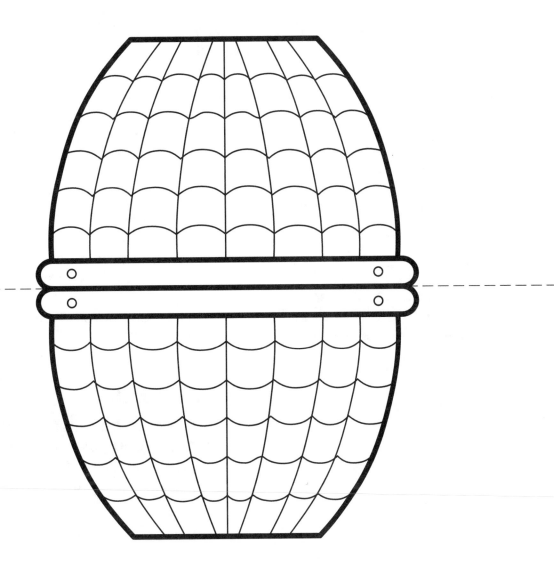

Before the Lesson

Have children bring umbrellas from home. Attach tags for identification.

Make copies of the umbrella poem on the right, one for each child.

Have on Hand

9" x 12" white construction paper
red, orange, yellow, green, blue and
   purple construction paper cut into
   6" x 9" pieces
construction paper scraps
crayons
scissors
glue

Read Aloud

Umbrella by Taro Yashima
Listen to *Yellow Umbrella* by Jae-Soo Liu
(a wordless picture book with musical CD;
   Korean song at end of music)

Talk About

As you listen to *Yellow Umbrella*, have children predict where the people are going. Write the colors of the rainbow in order on the chalkboard: red, orange, yellow, green, blue, purple. Read the color words together. Ask: "Which color begins with "r"? Which color ends in "n"? Which color has two "p" sounds?"

Teach children this short poem:

> Umbrellas come in many colors—
> Red, green, yellow and blue.
> When the rain comes falling down
> I'll share my umbrella with you.

Have the children share their umbrellas with the class. Look at the colors and designs.

Kids Create

• Children draw themselves on white paper and cut out the figures.

• Draw an umbrella on colored construction paper and cut it out.

• Draw an umbrella handle on scrap paper and cut it out.

• Glue the umbrella handle to one hand; glue the umbrella to the handle.

• Decorate the umbrella with colored construction paper scraps.

• Glue a copy of the poem on the paper.

U is for Ukulele

Uu

Before the Lesson

Trace the letter U patterns on pages 106-107 on the bottom of tagboard for each child.

Cut yarn into 15" lengths.

Have on Hand

letter U pattern
tagboard cut into 9" x 18" pieces, one per
    child
yarn
crayons
scissors
tape

Read Aloud

Abiyoyo by Pete Seeger
    (available as a book or book with CD)

Talk About

Review the South African folktale story-song with children, asking these questions: What instrument did the boy play? When the boy played his ukulele, what did the giant do? How do you think the giant felt as he was dancing? Why? How did the boy's father make the giant disappear?

Talk about the long u sound in the word *ukulele* and the letter u that makes the sound. Write other words with the long u sound on the chalkboard: *use, cute, huge, blue, flute* and *human*.

Note: There are many other words where the long u sound is made by "oo" as in *food* and "ew" as in *news.* Introduce words where only the letter "u" makes the long u sound.

Tell children they will be making ukuleles from the letter U. Show them how to add the rest of the body and the neck to make the tagboard U look like a ukulele.

Kids Create

• Color the ukulele pieces and cut them out.

• Glue the ukulele together.

• Tape three to four pieces of yarn on the ukulele for the strings.

• Children "play" their finished ukuleles as they sing the "Abiyoyo" song from the book.

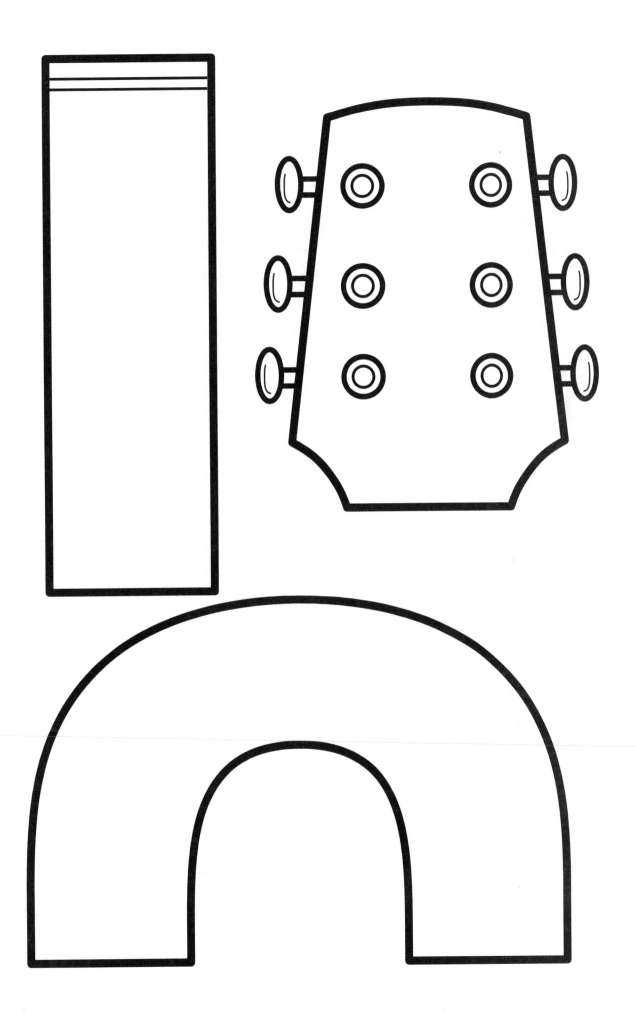

U is in sUn

Uu

Before the Lesson

Type or write the five sun facts at the bottom of this page and reproduce them for each child. Separate each sentence with a line for cutting. Letters should be small enough so each sentence will fit on a child's handprint.

Have on Hand

9" squares of yellow construction paper
4¹/₂" x 6" pieces of orange construction
    paper; five per child
crayons
scissors
glue

Read Aloud

The Sun: Our Nearest Star
    by Franklyn Mansfield Branley

Talk About

Write these facts about the sun on chart paper and discuss them with children:

- The sun is a star.
- The sun is made up of hot gases.
- The sun gives us heat and light.
- The sun helps plants grow.
- The sun is larger than the Earth.

Kids Create

- Draw a sun on yellow construction paper and cut it out.
- Help each child trace his or her hand on five pieces of orange construction paper.
- Cut out the handprints and glue them around the outside of the sun.
- Cut out each fact sentence and glue it on a handprint.
- Draw a face on the sun.

V is for Volcano

Vv

Before the Lesson

Divide the clay evenly.

Divide Crayola Model Magic™ evenly.

Fill a paper cup for each child with even amounts of vinegar and water, adding a couple of drops of red food coloring.

Have on Hand

plastic bowl and a piece of clay for each
  child
red food coloring, vinegar and water for
  each child
measuring cups
Crayola Model Magic™
red, orange, yellow, black and brown
  tissue paper cut into 1¹/₂" x 5" strips
red, orange, black and brown permanent
  markers
paper cups

Read Aloud

The Best Book of Volcanoes
  by Simon Adams
Rocking and Rolling by Philip Steele

Talk About

Children will be fascinated when they make and see a mini version of how a volcano erupts. Each child places a mound of clay in a plastic bowl, shapes it into a volcano and sprinkles one tablespoon of baking soda on it. Let them slowly pour the vinegar and water solution over the clay and watch the eruption!

After this activity, have children share what they think they know about volcanoes. Write their ideas on the chalkboard or on chart paper.

Kids Create

• Use Crayola Model Magic™ to make a volcano and let it dry.

• Color the volcano. Use red and orange markers to draw hot lava.

• Arrange and attach tissue paper strips to make it look like the volcano is erupting. Display the completed volcano with those of the rest of the class.

V is for **V**iolets in **V**ases

Vv

Before the Lesson

Assign children to work in groups of three to four.

Write the word *violets* and the numbers from 10 to 100 by 10s on the chalkboard.

Have on Hand

12" x 18" construction paper
9" x 12" construction paper
3" squares of purple construction paper or tissue paper
1" squares of yellow construction paper
dot markers
crayons
scissors
glue
real violets

Read Aloud

Planting a Rainbow by Lois Ehlert

Talk About

Review the sound of V and talk about the color and shape of violets. Show the children a few violets from a florist or a garden.

Kids Create

Working as a group:

• One child draws a large vase on the 9" x 12" paper and cuts it out.

• Another child writes the word *violets* on the vase and glues it onto the 12" x 18" construction paper.

• Children draw 10 violets, 10, on purple paper and cut them out.

• Children draw circles on yellow paper. Counting by 10s, they write the numbers from 10 to 100 on the circles and cut them out.

• Glue one yellow circle in the center of each violet.

• Arrange the violets on the large paper in order from left to right.

• Draw stems with green crayons and decorate them with crayons and dot markers.

V is for Vehicle

Vv

Before the Lesson

Set up a painting area in the classroom.

Create a sentence strip and reproduce it for each child.
"I like to _____ in my vehicle."

Have on Hand

paints
brushes
painting paper
pencils

Read Aloud

William the Vehicle King
    by Laura P. Newton
Cars and Trucks and Things That Go
    by Richard Scarry
My First Jumbo Book of Things That Go
    by Melanie Gerth

Talk About

Talk about the word *vehicle* and its meaning. Create a list of vehicles as children name them.

Kids Create

• Children paint pictures of their favorite vehicles.

• Complete the sentence strip and glue it on the picture.

• Children show their paintings.

• How many children painted cars? Trucks? Tractors? Trains? Busses? Taxis? Motorcycles?

I like to ___plow the fields___ in my vehicle.

W is for Mrs. Wishy-Washy

Ww

Before the Lesson

Complete the sentence to make a sample tub for children to copy.

Have on Hand

1 copy of tub pattern on page 113 for each child
12" x 18" construction paper
pencils
scissors
glue
colored pencils

Read Aloud

Mrs. Wishy-Washy's Farm by Joy Cowley

Talk About

Review the sound of W in Mrs. Wishy-Washy's name. Ask children to come up with other words that begin with W. Discuss why the animals left Mrs. Wishy-Washy's farm. Have the children list different items she could wash in her tub while the animals were gone. Show your sample and tell the children to fill in the sentence on the tub:

(child's name)'s Tub

(A/The) (name of item in the tub)

is (in) (the) tub.

Kids Create

- Help children fill in the names of the items and the sight words *in* and *a* or *the* on the tub pattern.
- Cut out the tub and glue it on the large sheet of construction paper.
- The children draw themselves in the tub with the items they put in the tub.
- Children share their work with the class.

_____'s Tub

__ __ _____

is _____ _____ tub.

_____'s Tub

__ __ _____

is _____ _____ tub.

W is for Wagon

Ww

Before the Lesson

Type the following sentence and reproduce it for each child on the bottom of 11" x 17" white paper:
"A _____ and a _____ are in my wagon."

Have on Hand

11" x 17" white paper
5" squares of black construction paper, two per child
4 1/2" x 12" construction paper, one per child
photos of different kinds of wagons
paper scraps
crayons
scissors
glue

Read Aloud

Dragon in a Wagon by Lynley Dodd

A bat and a
hat are in my wagon.

Talk About

Review the story and have the children listen for the rhyming words on each page. Make a list of rhyming items that could be in the wagon—mittens/kittens, hat/bat. Talk about what wagons are used for. How is a wagon different from other vehicles? What are some different kinds of wagons? Show photos of several different wagons— a covered wagon, a toy wagon, a wagon being pushed, a wagon being pulled.

Kids Create

- Children draw wagons on the 4 1/2" x 12" paper.
- Draw two wheels on black squares and cut them out.
- Glue the wagon and wheels on the white paper.
- Make a handle from scrap paper and glue it to the wagon.
- Draw two rhyming items in the wagon.
- Complete the sentence by writing what is in the wagon.

114

W is for Willoughby Wallaby Woo

Before the Lesson

Make a sentence strip and copy it for each child.
"Willoughby, Wallaby _____
An elephant sat on _____."

Copy the elephant pattern on construction paper.

Have on Hand

copies of elephant pattern on page 116
9" x 12" white construction paper
sentence strips
crayons
scissors
glue

Read Aloud

When We Were Very Young by A.A. Milne

Willoughby, Wallaby _Matthew_
An elephant sat on _Matthew_ .

Talk About

Considered a classic for generations, A.A. Milne's lilting and silly collection of verses about pets, kings, queens, games and pirates is still entertaining for young learners. Read some of the verses and have children memorize one or two.

Listen to the song "Willoughby Wallaby Woo" by Raffi on the CD *Singable Songs for the Very Young: Great with a Peanut Butter Sandwich*. (Although the title mentions a wallaby, the silly song is about an elephant.) After hearing the song, sing it without the tape and use the name of each child in your class in place of the names used in the song.

Kids Create

- Children color and cut out the elephant.
- Children draw themselves lying down and cut out the figures.
- They fill in the W word on the top line of the sentence strip. The word should rhyme with the child's name. They fill in their own name on the bottom line.
- Glue the elephant so it looks like it is sitting on them.
- Glue the sentence strip beneath the picture.

X is in TaXi

Taxi

Xx

Before the Lesson

Make a blackline master of the entire taxi and copy on 12" x 18" yellow paper, one for each child.

Create a sentence starter and copy it for each child. (Example: Taxi, taxi, take me to the red barn.)
"Taxi, taxi, take me to the _____ (color word) _____ (place)."

Have on Hand

copies of two-page taxi patterns on pages 118-119 on 12" x 18" paper
yellow construction paper
9" x 12" construction paper to match color words
crayons
scissors
pencils
glue

Read Aloud

Tina's Taxi by Betsy Franco
Maxi the Hero by Debra and Sal Barracca

Talk About

If your children live in a metropolitan area where they have been in a taxi, have them tell about the experience. How is it different from riding in a car? Display and review color words.

Kids Create

• Each child draws a driver and a passenger in the taxi and cuts it out.

• Draw where the taxis are going on 9" x 12" paper and cut it out.

• Finish the sentence by filling in a color word and the name of the place the taxi is going. (The color word should match the color of the cut-out place.)

Taxi, taxi, take me to the white house

Taxi

118

Taxi

X is in BoX

Xx

Before the Lesson

Write the word *box* on the board.

Type "There are _____ _____ in my box." at the top of 8½" x 11" white paper and copy for each child.

Make a sample as shown below for the children to follow.

Have on Hand

8½" x 11" white paper
6" x 9" construction paper
crayons
scissors
clear tape

Read Aloud

How Many Bugs in a Box
   by David A. Carter

Talk About

Display and review number words 1-10. Have children listen for the X sound at the end of *box*. What other words have an X in them? *taxi, wax, Max, fox, xylophone.* Talk about things other than bugs that could be in a box.

Kids Create

• Children write the word *box* on the 6" x 9" paper.

• Help them to tape down the 6" x 9" paper on the white paper below the sentence. (Tape only at the top.)

• Lift the paper and draw what is in the box on the white paper.

• Finish the sentence, filling in the number word and the name of the items in the box.

Y is for Yuck

Yy

Before the Lesson

Type the sentence "I put _____ in my yuck soup." on 8½" x 11" white paper and reproduce it for each child.

Have on Hand

digital camera
chef's hat
large soup pot
12" x 18" green construction paper
6" x 12" white construction paper
8½" x 11" white paper
crayons
glue

Read Aloud

Yuck! By Mick Manning

Talk About

Review the different yucky items that the animals in the book ate. Invite the children to share things they would never want to eat. Tell them that they will be making "yuck soup." Have the children brainstorm items they would like to put in the yuck soup.

Kids Create

• On the 6" x 12" paper, children each draw a yucky item to put in the soup pot and cut it out. Then let each child put on the chef's hat and take a photo of him or her putting the item in the soup pot.

• Children draw themselves putting the yucky item in the pot.

• Finish the sentence with the name of the item you put in the soup.

When the children are finished, glue each child's drawing beside his or her photo on green construction paper. Display them in an area of the school for all to see.

Y is for Yacht

Yy

Before the Lesson

Show photos of the inside and outside of yachts for children to copy.

Cover a long table with blue paper.

Have on Hand

3" x 11" pieces of white tagboard
star stickers
craft sticks
pipe cleaners
clear tape
craft foam letters
large piece of blue butcher paper or
   construction paper

Read Aloud

Kayaking, Canoeing, Rowing and Yachting
   by Christin Ditchfield

Before reading the book, ask the children what they think a yacht is. Write their responses on the chalkboard.

Talk About

After reading the section on yachts and looking at the yacht photos, review children's earlier answers. Ask the same question and record their new responses. Have them listen for the Y sound in *yacht* and *kayak*. Say other words with the Y sound and write them on chart paper: *you, yourself, yellow, yesterday, yawn, young* and *yard*.

Kids Create

• Place two 3" x 11" strips of tagboard together end-to-end and tape the ends together.

• Form an oval shape at the open end by overlapping the tagboard and taping them together keeping the oval shape of a yacht.

• Use tagboard scraps to make rooms on the yacht.

• Each glues foam letters that stand for his or her name on the side of the yacht.

• Add windows, railings and other boat details with pipe cleaners and star stickers.

• Make people using craft sticks and tape and put them on the yacht.

• Arrange the yachts on the blue paper-covered table.

Y is for Yo-Yo

Before the Lesson

Write *What Comes Next?* at the top of one piece of yellow paper.

Using a marker, write three or four numbers from 1-20 in random order on the left side of each piece of yellow paper. Leave enough space between the numbers for each child to glue a yo-yo. Draw a horizontal line next to each number where the children will glue the yo-yo.

Reproduce page 124 for each child. Write the numbers 1-20 on each yo-yo with a marker.

Have on Hand

several sheets of 12" x 18" yellow
 construction paper
6" lengths of yarn, one per child
permanent markers
crayons
scissors
glue
clear tape

Read Aloud

The Little Book of Yo-Yo's by Professor Yo-Yo
The Klutz Yo-Yo Book by the Editors of *Klutz*

Talk About

Talk about yo-yos and, if possible, bring one to show. Demonstrate how it works. Explain that yo-yos were popular outdoor toys many years ago. Allow children to try using the yo-yo. Review the sound of Y in *yo-yo* and review the numbers 1-20. Say a number and have a child tell the numbers that come next.

Kids Create

• Color one yo-yo, cut it out and glue a piece of yarn to the edge.

• Glue or tape a yo-yo next to the number it follows on the number page.

If you have more than 20 children in your class, increase the number to 25 or higher as needed.

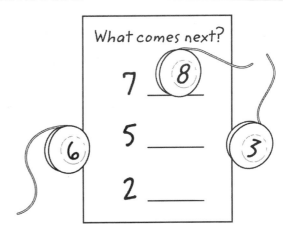

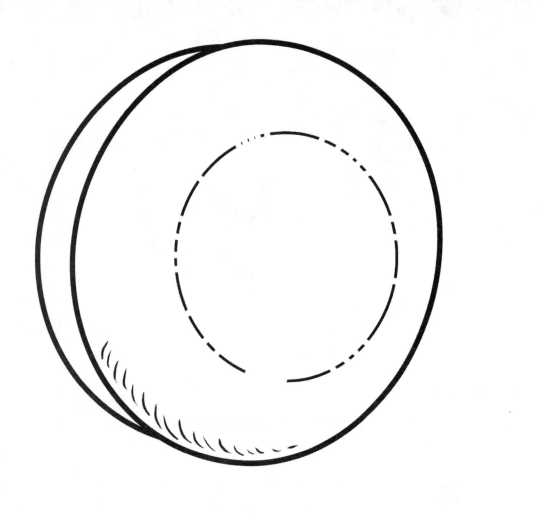

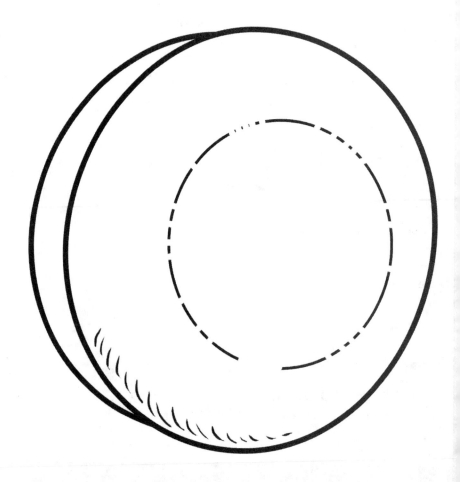

124

Z is for Zipper

Zz

Before the Lesson

Write *How Many Zippers Are You Wearing?* at the top of a piece of chart paper.

Write the numbers 0 to 8+ along the left side of the chart paper. Leave enough space between numbers for the children to attach their Post-It™ numbers.

Have on Hand

chart paper
Post-It™ notes, one per child

Read Aloud

Zack's Zippers by Cecilia Minden and Joanne Meier

Talk About

Before reading the story, plan a zipper day with your class. Send a note to parents asking that on a specific day their children wear clothing with as many zippers as possible and each bring in one non-clothing item with a zipper. Let the children stand and count the number of zippers they are wearing. Talk about other items such as luggage and handbags that have zippers on them. Have children share the zippered items they brought.

Kids Create

• Each child recounts the number of zippers he or she is wearing, then writes the number on a Post-It™ note and hangs the number beside the appropriate number on the graph.

• After everyone has had a turn, ask questions: Which row has the most zippers? The least? Are there any rows with zero zippers? If we add rows three and four together, how many zippers are there? Who wants to guess how many zippers are on the graph? Count to see if anyone guessed the exact number or who came the closest.

Before the Lesson

In large bold letters print or type on the computer each child's "Z" name (changing the first letter of the name to Z). Cut the letters apart, mix them up and put them in a plastic zip-type bag.

Have on Hand

6" x 18" pieces of construction paper, one per child
crayons
stickers
glue
sequins
large rubber playground ball

Read Aloud

A My Name Is Alice by Jane Bayer

Talk About

Review the Z sound and list several words on the chalkboard that begin with Z—*zoo, Zachary, zebra, zero, zigzag, zipper, zookeeper*. After reading the book, tell the children you are going to play a name game in which everyone's name will start with Z. Let each child practice saying his or her name, replacing the initial sound with Z—Colin would be Zolin, Moriah would be Zoriah, Bennett would be Zennett, etc. (Note: Zachary would remain Zachary.) To play the game, call out a child's Z name and toss a large playground ball to him or her. The child catches the ball, says a word that begins with Z and tosses the ball back to the teacher.

Kids Create

- Children put the letters of their Z name in order and glue them on construction paper.
- Decorate the paper with stickers and sequins.
- Add the names to the bulletin board titled "Our Zany Z Names."

Z is in BuZZing Bees

BUZZ

Zz

Before the Lesson

Write the following list of words that belong to the same word family on the chalkboard:

bug	far	dot	bit
rug	car	pot	hit
mug	jar	hot	fit

Draw an oval on the yellow paper for the bee's body for each child.

Using a black marker, label the bottom of each bee's body with one of these two-letter sounds: ar, it, ot, ug.

Reproduce page 128 for each child.

Have on Hand

copies of the words on page 128
9" x 12" yellow construction paper
3" x 6" black construction paper,
    two for each child
crayons
glue
black marker
fasteners/brads, two for each child

Read Aloud

Buzz Said the Bee
    by Wendy Cheyette Lewison

Talk About

Help the children read and hear the ending sounds in each word family on the chalkboard.

Kids Create

- Choose a bee body, add black stripes and a face and cut it out in an oval shape.
- Draw two wings on the black paper and cut them out.
- Attach the wings to the bee with fasteners or brads.
- Make a stinger with paper scraps you have left, cut it out and glue it on the bee.
- Read the two-letter sound on the bee and cut the words from the word list that end with the same two letters.
- Glue the words on the bee, then read the words to a friend and the teacher.

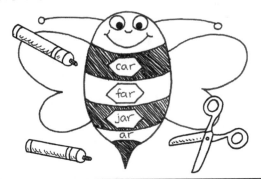

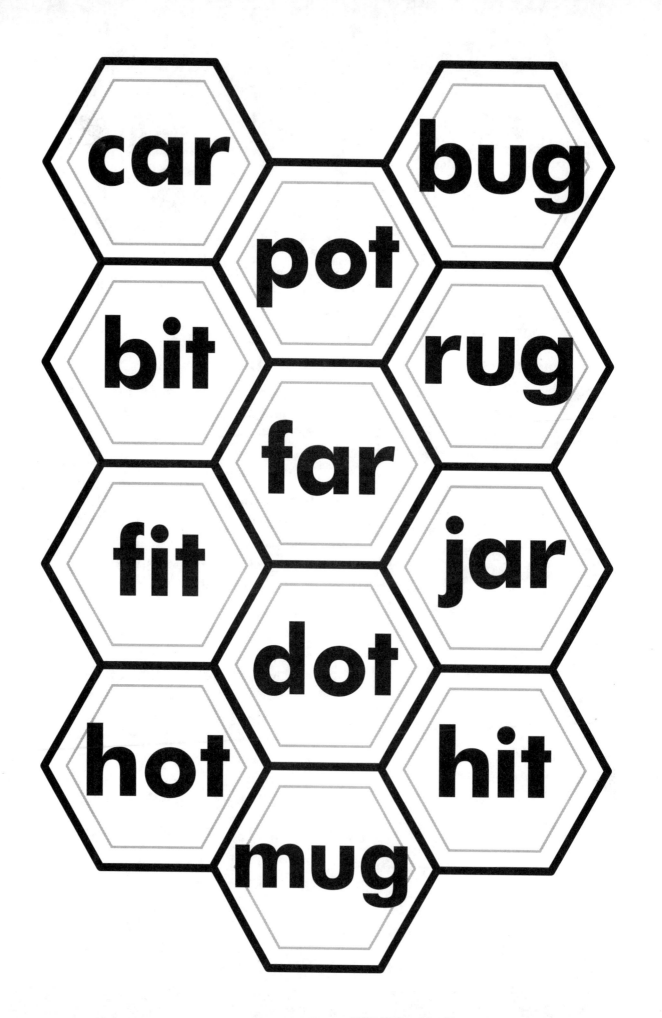